Let's Make Some

LUNCH

Recipes Made with Love for Everyone

Let's Make Some LUNCH

Recipes Made with Love for Everyone

Sulhee Jessica Woo

Publisher Mike Sanders
Art & Design Director William Thomas
Editorial Director Ann Barton
Senior Editor Olivia Peluso
Senior Designer Jessica Lee
Photographer Ciarra Siller
Food Stylist Marcella Capasso
Recipe Testers Molly Adams, Mary Dodd,
Patricia Sebben Malone, Lisa Nicklin
Proofreaders Christina Guthrie, Mira S. Park
Indexer Beverlee Day

First American Edition, 2024
Published in the United States by DK Publishing
1745 Broadway, 20th Floor, New York, NY 10019

The authorized representative in the EEA is Dorling Kindersley
Verlag GmbH. Arnulfstr. 124, 80636 Munich, Germany

A catalog record for this book
is available from the Library of Congress.
ISBN 978-0-7440-9301-8

DK books are available at special discounts when purchased
in bulk for sales promotions, premiums, fund-raising, or
educational use. For details, contact SpecialSales@dk.com

Printed and bound in China

www.dk.com

MIX
Paper | Supporting
responsible forestry
FSC™ C018179

This book was made with Forest
Stewardship Council™ certified
paper – one small step in DK's
commitment to a sustainable future.
Learn more at
www.dk.com/uk/information/sustainability

CONTENTS

INTRODUCTION

Hey guys!

I'm Sulhee Jessica Woo, but many know me as the Bento Box Queen. I'm a self-taught home cook and proud mother of three daughters: Adeline, Maxine, and Olive. I love making their lunches and packing them in fun and creative ways. One day, I came up with the idea to document what I was packing in their lunch boxes on the internet. To my surprise, people began to resonate with my videos, leading to an inflow of questions, messages, and comments about everything from the recipes themselves to the products I use to make each lunch special.

In early 2020, my videos went viral, and I have been deeply moved by the personal reactions to my videos. Reading your stories and messages has truly meant the world to me. It's crazy to think that I now have the privilege of making lunches for an online community of millions of people. It is truly an honor to be a part of so many lives and to share this passion with all of you.

When I create short-form food content, I have to fit everything into 60 seconds or less. But in this book, I can really expand on my experiences and techniques, guiding you through each step. My hope is that you'll find inspiration here to take time for the little things in life, like making heart-shaped sandwiches, cutting fruit into flowers, or writing love notes sealed with a kiss.

This book is perfect for anyone looking to try new and adventurous recipes for their loved ones. Whether it's a quick, easy-to-make lunch or a leisurely meal spent cooking with your family, these recipes are versatile and can be used for any meal. Leftovers (in my opinion) make the best lunches!

I hope this book becomes a treasured addition to your collection, providing you with sweet and nostalgic moments while preparing thoughtful lunches for those you love.

Consider me your lunch fairy godmother.

My first viral lunch!

A LOVE OF FOOD AND ART

Since 2011, I have been creating content about the things I'm passionate about. I've shared outfit videos, shopping hauls, and food and drink recipes while juggling multiple jobs as a makeup artist, cocktail server, and sales associate at a luxury lingerie company. Also in 2011, I became a mother when my daughter Adeline was born. After my second daughter, Maxine, was born in 2014, I became a single parent, making it difficult for me to continue creating. Nonetheless, I've always cherished the idea of capturing precious moments through the lens of a camera.

Food has always been another one of my passions. For as long as I can remember, I've loved trying new cuisines and savoring the delicious dishes my mommy cooked for me. I have always loved everything that food represents, especially how it brings people together. My umma used to tell me that even as a baby, I would have an expression of pure bliss whenever someone would bring me a plate of food. She instilled in me a love for diverse cuisine, and we bonded over our shared love for cooking and enjoying meals together. The combination of food and art is my ultimate happy place, and I stumbled upon it while preparing lunch for my children.

Like many other parents, I began making packed lunches out of necessity when Adeline started kindergarten. This was the first time we were apart from each other almost every day—a significant milestone in both our lives. As a mom, it was important for me to give her the space to grow and develop her own interests. But expressing my love through acts of service has always been my specialty, and cooking and entertaining have become my love language. With Adeline starting school, not being able to feed her myself became a major concern for me: Would she have enough food? Would she have enough time to eat? What if she didn't like what I had packed and went hungry all day?

Addy on her first day of kindergarten

One of the first lunches I made for Addy

A special Valentine's Day lunch! ALL candy, ha!

After my divorce, I started cooking more often. My main motivation was to introduce my daughter to different traditional cuisines and encourage her to expand her taste buds. I wanted to show her that food should be a source of comfort in her life and not something to be afraid of (one major challenge for me was making vegetables more appealing to her, and I found creative ways to do that!). Every day, I made her lunch with love and included a note to let her know how much she meant to me.

Making her lunch became a passion, and I became quite skilled at it. To keep things exciting, I challenged myself to be more creative and surprise her with something yummy and cute every day of the week. Though I could have seen this as a chore, it became a mindfulness task for me. It's amazing how something as simple as making lunch can turn into an act of love and creativity.

Crafting adorable and delicious lunches with love has brought me to this point, and I am thrilled and grateful to have you as a reader. In this book, I share the secrets to creating delightful lunches.

Now, lunchtime will never be boring! I've included recipes for every craving, that can be enjoyed at any time of day: "breakfast for lunch," classic lunchtime sandwiches, and dinner leftover-inspired meals. I love to introduce my girls to cuisines from around the world, so you'll find my globally inspired recipes starting on page 168. To supplement your lunch-making journey, use my cooking staples to make your own rice, broth, and more! Enjoy the process, embrace the fun, and let your affection flow into every detail of your lunch-making routine!

XOXO,

Jess

LUNCH 101

MY FAVORITE LUNCH BOXES

Packing a delicious and well-balanced meal for yourself or your loved ones is made infinitely easier with the right lunch box. I prefer to use a variety of lunch boxes for different types of food, and each serves a distinct purpose. Initially, when preparing lunches for Addy, I simply made use of plastic containers I had lying around. However, more recently, and especially after my lunch videos gained popularity, many diverse lunch boxes have become available. Below are some of my top picks, along with the reasons why I frequently reach for them.

STAINLESS STEEL

Stainless steel lunch boxes have become increasingly popular in recent years due to their durability and eco-friendliness. They are a great choice if you prioritize durability, eco-friendliness, and hygiene.

Bentgo stainless steel lunch boxes

PROS:

1. **Durable:** Stainless steel is highly durable and can withstand rough handling, making it ideal for daily use.
2. **Eco-friendly:** Stainless steel is recyclable, while plastic lunch boxes often end up in landfills.
3. **Hygienic:** Stainless steel does not retain odors or flavors from previous meals, making it easy to clean and maintain.
4. **Aesthetically pleasing:** Stainless steel lunch boxes have a stylish, sleek, and modern appearance.

CONS:

1. **Cost:** Stainless steel lunch boxes can be more expensive than plastic or fabric options.
2. **Heavy:** Stainless steel is heavier than plastic, which may make it inconvenient to carry around all day.
3. **Not microwave-safe:** Unlike plastic, stainless steel is not microwave-safe, so you will need to transfer your food to a microwave-safe container before reheating.

RICE HUSK

Rice husk lunch boxes are an eco-friendlier alternative to plastic. They are both durable and lightweight.

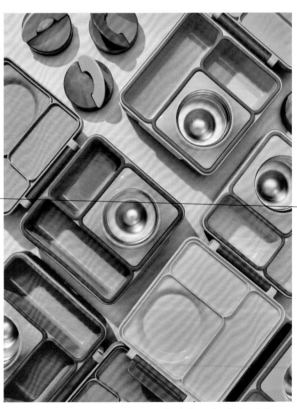
OmieBox plastic lunch boxes

Yumbox plastic lunch boxes

CONS:

1. **Might not be dishwasher safe:** Some rice husk lunch boxes are not dishwasher safe, which means you will need to wash them by hand.

2. **May retain odors:** Depending on the materials used, rice husk boxes may retain odors from previous meals.

3. **May stain easily:** Rice husk lunch boxes may stain easily, especially if they come into contact with colorful foods like tomato sauce.

PLASTIC

Plastic lunch boxes are one of the most popular options, as they are the most practical and economical. There is a huge range of designs, sizes, and price points to choose from. I love that they are lightweight for the little ones to carry around, and the built-in organizers make it easy to assemble lunches every day.

PROS:

1. **Affordable:** Plastic lunch boxes are generally very affordable, making them an accessible option for many.

2. **Lightweight:** Plastic is a lightweight material, which makes it easy to carry around all day.

3. **Variety of designs:** Plastic lunch boxes come in a wide variety of designs, colors, and sizes, making it easy to find one that suits your needs.

4. **Dishwasher-safe:** Most plastic lunch boxes are dishwasher safe, which makes cleaning up after meals quick and convenient.

CONS:

1. **Not eco-friendly:** Plastic is not biodegradable, and many plastic containers end up in landfills, where they can take hundreds of years to break down.

2. **May retain odors:** Plastic containers may retain odors from previous meals, even after washing.

3. **Less durable:** Compared to metal or other materials, plastic is less durable and can crack or break if dropped or mishandled.

4. **May contain harmful chemicals:** Some plastic containers may contain harmful chemicals like BPA, which can leach into your food over time.

PROS:

1. **Eco-friendly:** Rice husks are a byproduct of rice production and would otherwise be discarded as waste. Using these husks for lunch boxes helps reduce waste and is more sustainable than disposable options.

2. **Durable:** Rice husk lunch boxes can withstand daily use, making them a good investment.

3. **Lightweight:** Rice husk lunch boxes are lightweight and easy to carry around.

4. **Microwave-safe:** Many rice husk lunch boxes are microwave-safe, which makes it convenient to reheat your food.

BAMBOO AND WOOD

Great for picnics and lunches that will be eaten sooner rather than later. They are perfect for capturing a picture of your finished masterpiece. Sandwiches, snacks, and easy finger foods fit best.

PROS:

1. **Sustainable:** Bamboo is a renewable resource that grows quickly and doesn't require replanting.

2. **Lightweight:** Bamboo lunch boxes are typically lighter than their wood counterparts, making them easier to carry around.

3. **Durable:** Bamboo is naturally strong and resistant to scratches and dents.

4. **Aesthetics:** Wood lunch boxes have a unique and stylish appearance that adds character and warmth to your lunchtime routine.

CONS:

1. **Limited design options:** Bamboo lunch boxes may not come in as many design options as wood ones, since bamboo isn't as commonly used.

2. **Water-absorbent:** Bamboo and wood lunch boxes can absorb water, which may make them difficult to clean or cause mold growth if not properly cared for.

3. **Can crack or split:** While bamboo is durable, it can still crack or split, especially if dropped.

4. **Not dishwasher safe:** Bamboo and wood lunch boxes are usually not dishwasher safe.

Explore the world of lunch boxes and find out what works best for you! And remember, no matter which lunch box you choose, your lunches will always be packed with love. So get creative, make nutritious choices, and let's embark on this delicious journey!

Bento&co wooden lunch boxes

TOOLS AND ADORNMENTS

Creating a special lunch requires the right tools and adornments. Like an artist uses brushes and paints to create a masterpiece, I have my go-to items that help me make lunches extra special. Here are a few of my favorites.

FOOD PICKS

Cute little food picks are an adorable addition to any home kitchen or dining table. These miniature utensils come in a variety of shapes, sizes, and colors, adding a playful touch to your meals.

Food picks can be used to skewer fruits, vegetables, meats, cheese, and other bite-size snacks, making them easier to handle and eat. They also add a little fun to a party or gathering, an easy way for you to grab a quick snack without having to use your hands.

Whether you're serving appetizers at a dinner party, packing a lunch box, or just snacking on some fresh veggies, cute little food picks are a charming way to elevate your eating experience.

FOOD SHAPE CUTTERS

Fun food shape cutters are a great way to make mealtime more exciting and enjoyable for both kids and adults. These cutters come in a variety of shapes and sizes, allowing you to create fun and creative designs with your favorite foods. Use them to cut sandwiches, fruits, vegetables, cheese, and even cookies.

Not only do these cutters make food look more visually appealing, but they can also encourage picky eaters to try new foods. Kids often enjoy eating foods that are shaped like their favorite characters or objects. It's a great way to get them excited about healthy foods that they may not have otherwise wanted to try. They are also a great tool for themed parties or events. You could use animal-shaped cutters for a safari-themed party or heart-shaped cutters for Valentine's Day.

INSULATED LUNCH BAGS

Insulated lunch bags are designed to keep your food and drinks at the right temperature for an extended period. They are commonly made of a durable material,

such as polyester, nylon, or neoprene, and have an insulated layer inside that helps maintain the temperature.

Insulated lunch bags have many benefits. They:

- Keep food fresh and at the right temperature,
- Prevent spills and leaks,
- Are durable and easy to clean,
- Are an eco-friendly alternative to disposable containers,
- Have multiple compartments for organizing food and drinks, and
- Are portable and convenient for on-the-go meals.

When choosing an insulated lunch bag, consider its size, durability, insulation quality, and ease of cleaning. Choose a size that can fit all your food and drink containers, and make sure that the bag is made of a durable material that can withstand daily use.

TWEEZERS AND SCISSORS

Tweezers are great for picking up small items like seeds, berries, or garnishes and placing them precisely on top of dishes. They can also be used to remove any unwanted pieces from fruits or vegetables.

Micro-tip scissors are perfect for cutting delicate items like nori or thinly sliced meats and great for creating decorative shapes out of ingredients like cheese. They can truly make a big difference in the presentation and quality of your lunchtime creations.

SILICONE CUPS

These reusable and flexible containers are great for holding snacks, fruit, and small portions. They can keep your lunch separated and organized without the mess. They're oven-safe, so you can also use them to cook or bake!

RICE BALL MAKER

Rice balls are super fun to make, and kids love to eat them. Create mini rice balls with ease using this tool. Add a small amount of rice and give it a nice shake to create the perfect rice sphere.

FOOD FACE AND SHAPE PUNCHERS

These crafty punchers help create cute character faces. I like to use them on nori seaweed paper, just like a paper hole puncher.

ICE PACKS

I like to include ice packs to help maintain the temperature of perishable foods and prevent spoilage. Ice packs come in various sizes and can be placed inside lunch bags or coolers to help keep food fresh and safe to eat.

LUNCH NOTES

Small notes or cards are a special addition to make any lunch feel special. They can be personalized with a handwritten message or can be purchased premade in a variety of designs. I've included a few notecards at the end of the book so you can make your own, along with stickers to seal them with love.

PANTRY MUST-HAVES

In this section, I invite you to spark your culinary imagination and venture beyond your comfort zone by using items that are probably already in your pantry. I hope you feel empowered to make the most of what you have. Embrace unfamiliar ingredients to broaden your palate and unleash your creativity. Get ready to create your own signature dishes, and revel in the joy of endless culinary possibilities!

All-purpose flour

Almond milk (page 258)

Applesauce (page 51)

Artichoke hearts

Baking soda

Baking powder

Beans: black beans, kidney beans

Black olives

Bread crumbs: panko bread crumbs, plain bread crumbs

Broth & stock: beef broth (page 261), chicken stock (page 260), vegetable stock (page 259)

Cocoa powder

Cheese

Coconut: coconut milk, sweetened shredded coconut

Condensed milk

Coffee

Corn: canned corn, fresh corn, cornmeal, cornstarch, creamed corn, hominy

Croutons (page 135)

Food coloring: You can buy food coloring in stores or use natural food coloring, though natural food coloring may have a slight flavor. Beetroot juice can add a vibrant pink or red color to recipes, while hibiscus flowers create a rich magenta color when steeped in hot water. Carrot juice provides a subtle orange or yellow hue, and turmeric powder has a bright yellow color. Juiced spinach and kale produce a natural green coloring, while mashed or blended blueberries and blackberries create a purplish-blue color. Boiling red cabbage in water and using the liquid can produce shades of blue or purple, and lemon juice can create a pinkish hue.

Glutinous rice flour: Made from glutinous rice, glutinous rice flour is known for its sticky and elastic texture when cooked. It's commonly used in Asian cuisine and gluten-free baking.

Instant & active dry yeast

Noodles: The recipes in this book use several different types of noodles, including egg noodles, Thai flat rice noodles, Korean vermicelli, and Filipino bihon rice noodles.

Nori: Thin sheets of roasted seaweed are the perfect medium to cut and punch designs from, just like paper!

Nuts: almonds, pecans, roasted peanuts, walnuts

Pasta: Use your favorite pasta shapes in these recipes. Some of our faves are tricolor rotini, elbow macaroni, and shells.

Pickles: baby beets, daikon, dill pickles, ginger

Pineapple: canned pineapple, pineapple juice

Pizza sauce

Potato starch: Potato starch is a gluten-free white powder extracted from potatoes, commonly used as a thickening agent.

Pumpkin puree

Rice: I use good-quality, medium-grain jasmine white rice daily, but there are so many different types of rice I love. I started mixing quinoa and brown rice to get more protein into my little ones' meals, and it has been a hit. Try mixing different grains together!

For some recipes, you'll also need basmati or Arborio rice.

Rolled oats

Sauerkraut

Sago tapioca pearls: Tapioca pearls are chewy little balls often used in desserts. I love adding them to smoothies and slushies for a fun texture!

Seeds: chia seeds, pumpkin seeds, sunflower seeds

Sprinkles

Sprite: I use this as a meat tenderizer, and it adds a little bit of sweetness.

Tomatoes: canned crushed tomatoes, canned stewed tomatoes, sun-dried tomatoes in oil, tomato paste, tomato puree

OILS, CONDIMENTS, AND DRESSINGS

CONDIMENTS AND SAUCES

BBQ sauce

Buffalo sauce

Butter

Clamato juice: A drink made from a blend of tomato juice and clam

Let's Make Some Lunch

broth. It has a savory and slightly briny flavor. Add it to soups, stews, and sauces to enhance their flavors with a hint of seafood taste.

Dijon mustard

Fish sauce: A condiment commonly used in Southeast Asian cuisine. It's made by fermenting fish, usually anchovies or other small, saltwater fish, with sea salt. Fish sauce has a distinct umami flavor that adds depth and complexity to dishes. It is often used as a seasoning in stir-fries, soups, marinades, dipping sauces, and dressings. Use sparingly, as it can be quite potent.

Ginger-garlic paste

Honey and hot honey

Hot sauce

Japanese mayonnaise: Also known as Kewpie mayonnaise, this popular Japanese condiment is a creamy and rich mayonnaise that has a slightly sweeter and tangier flavor than Western mayonnaise. Japanese mayo is made with egg yolks, vinegar or rice vinegar, mustard, and sometimes a small amount of MSG.

Kecap manis: A sweet, thick Indonesian soy sauce. It is made from fermented soybeans, palm sugar, water, and spices. Use as a dipping sauce, marinade, or glaze for meats, poultry, seafood, vegetables, and noodles.

Ketchup

Mayonnaise

Miso paste: Made from fermented soybeans, along with rice or barley and salt, miso paste has a sweet, earthy, umami-rich flavor. It is commonly used in Japanese cuisine to make miso soup, but it's also a versatile ingredient for marinades, dressings, glazes, and sauces. It can be used to enhance the flavor of soups, stews, stir-fries, and even desserts. Miso paste is highly nutritious and rich in protein, vitamins, and minerals.

Oyster sauce: A thick, savory sauce made from oysters that are cooked and then simmered in water until their juices condense into a thick sauce. Oyster sauce has a rich umami flavor, with hints of sweetness and saltiness. It is often used in stir-fries, noodle dishes, marinades, and dipping sauces.

Peanut butter

Soy sauce: A staple in my kitchen, soy sauce adds flavor and saltiness to a variety of dishes. It's easy to pack in lunches (either with takeout packets or mini sauce bottles).

Sweet and sour sauce

Tamarind paste: A thick, dark brown paste made from the pulp of the tamarind fruit. It has a tangy and sour taste with a hint of sweetness. Tamarind paste is commonly used as a flavoring agent in various cuisines around the world. It is high in antioxidants and fiber, and it is believed to aid digestion, promote healthy skin, and help manage blood sugar levels.

Tempura dipping sauce (tentsuyu)

Worcestershire sauce

DRESSINGS

Blue cheese dressing

Caesar dressing

Italian dressing (page 135)

Ranch dressing (page 101)

OILS

Avocado oil

Coconut oil

Olive oil

Sesame oil: Toasted sesame oil adds a burst of nutty flavor to dressings, marinades, and dips. So yummy!

Vegetable oil

VINEGARS

Apple cider vinegar

Balsamic vinegar: Simmer in a small pan for a few minutes to make a balsamic glaze.

Rice vinegar: Made from fermented rice, rice vinegar is commonly used in Asian cuisine, particularly in Japanese, Chinese, and Korean dishes. It has a mild, slightly sweet flavor, making it popular for dressings, marinades, pickling, and dipping sauces.

SPICES AND SEASONINGS

BOUILLON

Beef bouillon

Beef dasida

Chicken bouillon

CHILES

Ancho chiles (dried)

Arbol chiles (dried)

Guajillo chiles

SPICES AND FLAVORINGS

Basil (dried)

Bay leaves

Black pepper

Cayenne

Coriander

Chili powder

Cinnamon

Cumin

Dill (dried)

Everything bagel seasoning

Garam masala

Gochugaru: A type of Korean chile pepper powder. It is commonly used in Korean cuisine to add spicy and smoky flavors to kimchi, stews, soups, and marinades.

Kosher salt

Li hing mui powder: Also known as plum powder, this is a popular seasoning in Hawaiian cuisine. It is made from dried and ground li hing mui, which are pickled and dried plums from China. Li hing mui powder has a unique sweet, salty, and tangy flavor. It is often sprinkled on fruits, candies, snacks, and even used in cocktails.

Mustard seeds

Nutmeg

Old Bay seasoning

Oregano (dried)

Pandan flavoring: Made from the leaves of the pandan plant. It adds a sweet, floral flavor and green color to dishes, and is commonly used in Southeast Asian cooking for its unique taste.

Paprika

Red chili powder

Red pepper flakes

Sesame seeds: Nutty in flavor, these seeds can be consumed in various forms, including raw, toasted, or ground into a paste (tahini). They are often sprinkled on top of bread, buns, or pastries to add a crunchy texture and enhance the flavor. Sesame seeds are also commonly used in sauces, dressings, marinades, and desserts.

Smoked paprika

Thyme (dried)

Turmeric

Vanilla extract

SUGARS

Granulated sugar

Light brown sugar

Palm sugar: A type of sweetener derived from the sap of palm trees. It is commonly used in Southeast Asian cuisine and is known for its rich flavor and caramel-like taste. I use the ones that come in blocks or disks.

Powdered sugar

PLAYLIST

I've curated a selection of my all-time favorite songs for you to enjoy while cooking these recipes. Happy listening!

LUNCH BOX SNACKS

I love to pack snacks for every lunch, so here is a list of ideas for completing your lunch! I like to add a little bit from each category to make a well-balanced meal and as a little pick-me-up treat to make my girls' days even sweeter. For the veggies, I either steam them or pack them raw with some ranch dressing (see page 101) on the side.

FRUIT

Applesauce (page 51)

Apples

Avocado

Bananas

Blackberries

Blueberries

Cantaloupe

Cherries

Cherry tomatoes

Cucumber

Figs

Goji berries

Grapes

Honeydew

Kiwi

Kumquats

Mango

Oranges

Pineapple

Pomegranate seeds

Raisins

Rambutan

Raspberries

Star fruit

Strawberries

Sweet peppers

Tangerines

Watermelon

VEGGIES

Artichokes

Asparagus

Baby bok choy

Baby carrots

Bell peppers

Blistered Teriyaki
    Shishito Peppers
    (page 125)

Broccoli

Cauliflower florets

Celery

Corn

Crispy Cauliflower Bites
    (page 101)

Edamame

Green beans

Kimchi

Parmesan Zucchini
    Fries (page 85)

Pickles

Potatoes

Sautéed Butter
    Mushrooms (page 63)

Sautéed Spinach
    (page 75)

Seaweed snacks

Snap peas

Sweet potatoes

PROTEIN SNACKS

Almonds

Beef sticks or jerky

Cashews

Cheese cubes or sticks

Chickpeas

Cottage cheese

Crunchy Nut Granola
    (page 66)

Hummus

Nut butter

Peanut butter puffs

Peanuts

Pecans

Perfect Boiled Eggs
    (page 257)

Pistachios

Protein bars

Tofu

Turkey bacon

Walnuts

Yogurt

SWEET & SAVORY SNACKS

Animal crackers

Brownies

Caramelized Banana
    Bread (page 67)

Chocolate

Cookies

Corn nuts

Crackers

Fig bars

Fruit Chips (page 262)

Fruit snacks

Homemade Tortilla
    Chips (page 145)

Marshmallows

Mini muffins and
    pastries

Parmesan crisps

Pita chips

Pocky

Popcorn

Potato chips

Pretzels

Pudding

Puffed rice chips

Pumpkin bread

Trail mix

Veggie Chips
    (page 263)

Wafer cookies

Yogurt-covered raisins

Yogurt drops

Zucchini bread

LUNCH FAQ

HOW DO YOU FIGURE OUT PORTION SIZES FOR LUNCH?

When determining portion sizes for kids' lunch, it's important to consider their age, activity level, and specific dietary needs. Here are some general guidelines.

1. Aim to include a variety of food groups, such as fruits, vegetables, grains, protein, and dairy.

2. Consider age-based recommendations: Guidelines may vary based on the child's age group. For example, preschoolers typically require smaller portions than older children.

3. Use your child's hand as a measuring tool: For younger kids, you can use their hand size to estimate portion sizes. For instance, one serving of vegetables could be the size of their fist, while a serving of protein (e.g., chicken or fish) should be about the size of their palm.

4. Balance macronutrients: Ensure that the lunch includes a good balance of carbohydrates, proteins, and healthy fats. Include foods like whole-grain bread or pasta, lean meats or plant-based proteins, and sources of healthy fats like nuts, seeds, or avocado.

5. Include adequate fruits and vegetables: Encourage kids to consume a variety of fruits and vegetables by including them in their lunch. Aim for one to two servings of fruit and at least one serving of vegetables per lunch.

6. Serve appropriate portion sizes of grains: Grains like rice, pasta, or bread should make up a quarter of the meal. Use measuring cups or scales if needed.

7. Be mindful of added sugars: Limit sugary beverages or desserts in lunch boxes and opt for healthier alternatives like water, milk, or yogurt.

Remember, these guidelines may vary depending on your child's individual needs and preferences. It is always a good idea to consult a health care professional or a registered dietitian for personalized advice.

HOW DO YOU KEEP YOUR LUNCHES WARM?

There are a few methods you can use to keep packed lunches warm:

1. Insulated lunch containers: High-quality insulated lunch boxes or containers specifically designed to keep food warm work best.

2. Thermos containers: Use a thermos container to keep hot foods warm. Before packing the food, preheat the thermos by filling it with boiling water for a few minutes, then empty it and immediately add the hot food. This helps maintain the temperature for longer.

3. Foil wrap and insulation: Wrap the hot food tightly with aluminum foil and place it inside an insulated lunch bag or wrap the container with a kitchen towel, securing it with rubber bands or clips. This extra layer of insulation helps retain the heat.

Remember to always follow food safety guidelines when preparing and storing food. Hot foods should be kept at a safe temperature (above 140°F/60°C) to prevent bacterial growth. Pack any accompanying cold items separately to maintain their freshness.

HOW DO YOU KEEP YOUR LUNCHES COOL?

Keeping lunches cool is essential to ensure food safety and maintain freshness when there isn't a refrigerator available. Here are some ways to keep lunches cool.

1. Insulated lunch containers: Insulated lunch boxes or cooler bags help keep the contents cool. These containers are designed to maintain a lower temperature and prevent heat transfer.

2. Ice packs or gel packs: Place reusable ice packs or gel packs inside the lunch box or cooler bag to keep food chilled. These packs stay colder for longer periods and can be refrozen for future use.

3. Frozen water bottles: Freeze water bottles overnight and use them as a dual-purpose cooling agent. They serve both as a cold source for keeping the food cool and can be consumed once thawed.

4. Freeze components of the lunch: Cut fruit or vegetables into bite-size pieces and freeze them in advance. These frozen pieces can act as edible ice packs and serve as a refreshing snack when thawed.

5. Layering and packing techniques: Strategically pack the lunch by layering cool ingredients on top of each other. For example, place a frozen juice box or yogurt next to the main dish to help maintain its temperature. You can also separate different food items into individual containers to prevent cross-contamination and maintain their respective temperatures.

6. Avoid high-risk foods on warm days: On hot days, consider avoiding highly perishable or temperature-sensitive foods like raw seafood, unpasteurized dairy products, or mayo-based dishes if you're unable to keep them properly chilled.

Remember, it is crucial to follow food safety guidelines and discard any perishable leftovers or uneaten food after a certain period (usually within two hours) to prevent foodborne illnesses.

HOW DO YOU KEEP FOOD CRISPY?

Keeping food crispy when packing a lunch can be a challenge, especially if the meal will sit for a while before being eaten. However, there are a few tips and techniques you can try to maintain crispiness.

1. Separate moist ingredients: Keep moist ingredients separate until it's time to eat. For example, pack dressings, sauces, or moist toppings in small containers or compartments within the lunchbox. This prevents them from making other components soggy.

2. Use paper towels or napkins: Place a layer of absorbent paper towel or napkin at the bottom of the container to absorb excess moisture and help prevent the food from becoming soggy.

3. Precook and cool fried foods: If you plan to include fried items like chicken tenders or crispy vegetables, cook them ahead of time and let them cool completely on a wire rack before packing. This helps retain their crispiness better than packing them while hot.

4. Pack using separate containers: When possible, pack crispy items separately from moist or saucy components. For instance, keep salads or fresh vegetables in one container and crunchy items like croutons or nuts in another. Assemble them just before eating to maintain their texture.

5. Ventilation or breathable packaging: When packing warm items like sandwiches, wraps, or baked goods, use containers or wrapping materials that allow some airflow. This helps prevent condensation and maintains crispness better than sealed containers.

6. Reheating: If a microwave or oven is available, pack certain items separately and reheat them right before eating to restore their crispness. For example, you could pack the filling and tortillas of a wrap separately and assemble and heat it when ready to eat.

Remember that some foods naturally lose their crispness over time, and it may not always be possible to maintain their initial level of crunchiness. But these tips can help optimize crispiness and improve the overall eating experience of these packed lunches.

WHAT DO YOU DO WITH THE CUTOUTS AND LEFTOVERS?

There are a few options for things you can do with your leftovers and cutout pieces of food after packing a lunch.

1. Repurpose them into new dishes: Get creative and transform leftover meats, vegetables, or grains into tasty stir-fries, salads, wraps, or omelets. Combine them with fresh ingredients to create exciting meals.

2. Make comforting soups or stews: Use your leftover cooked chicken, vegetables, or pasta to enhance a pot of flavorful soup or stew. This is a great way to utilize small portions of different ingredients.

3. Create satisfying grain bowls or salads: Utilize leftover grains like rice, quinoa, or couscous as a base and top them with chopped veggies, protein (such as cooked chicken or beans), and your favorite dressing to make delicious and nutritious grain bowls or salads.

4. Most days, I just eat them!

HOW LONG DOES FOOD LAST IN THE FRIDGE?

This depends on the type of food. Here are some general guidelines.

1. **Dairy products:** Milk can last for about a week after the "best by" date. Yogurt, sour cream, and cottage cheese can last for up to 2 weeks. Hard cheeses can last for several weeks.

2. **Meat and poultry:** Raw meat and poultry can be stored in the fridge for 1 to 2 days. Cooked meat and poultry can last for 3 to 4 days.

3. **Seafood:** Raw seafood should be consumed within 1 to 2 days. Cooked seafood can last for 3 to 4 days.

4. **Fruits and vegetables:** Most fresh fruits and vegetables can last for 3 to 5 days in the fridge. Leafy greens like lettuce and spinach may wilt sooner.

5. **Hard-boiled eggs:** Hard-boiled eggs can typically be stored in the refrigerator for up to 1 week. It is best to keep them in their shells to maintain freshness and prevent any potential contamination. To ensure the longest shelf life, store the eggs in a covered container or plastic bag to avoid absorbing odors from other foods in the fridge.

6. **Leftovers:** Leftovers should be consumed or refrigerated within 2 hours of cooking. They can typically last for 3 to 4 days in the fridge.

It's important to note that the freshness and quality of food can vary depending on factors like storage conditions and proper handling. Always use your judgment and rely on your senses (smell, appearance, and taste) to determine if food is still safe to eat.

WHERE DO YOU GET YOUR IDEAS AND HOW DO YOU STAY CREATIVE?

There are several ways you can find inspiration and stay creative when it comes to packing your lunches:

1. **Online recipe websites and blogs:** Explore popular cooking websites and food blogs that offer a variety of recipes specifically tailored for lunches and meal prep. They often provide step-by-step instructions, ingredient lists, and photos to inspire your creativity.

2. **Social media platforms:** Follow food-related accounts, chefs, and influencers on platforms like Instagram, Pinterest, or YouTube. They regularly share creative lunch box ideas, trendy recipes, and tips for meal planning.

3. **Cookbooks and magazines:** Browse through cookbooks (like this one!) or subscribe to culinary magazines that focus on healthy eating, meal prep, or lunch box ideas. These resources often provide diverse recipes and suggestions for putting together well-balanced meals.

4. **Experiment with new ingredients:** Try incorporating different ingredients, flavors, and textures to keep your lunches exciting. Explore new fruits, veggies, spices, herbs, grains, or proteins to add variety and enhance the taste of your meals.

5. **Plan ahead and brainstorm:** Take some time each week to plan your lunches in advance. Sit down and brainstorm ideas, considering your dietary preferences, any leftovers you may have, and the overall balance of nutrients you'd like to achieve.

6. I like to ask my kids and get them involved in what goes in their lunches. Getting them to participate in cooking and sharing ideas makes the lunch-making process a lot more fun!

Remember, staying creative is all about exploring new ideas, being open to experimentation, and enjoying the process of creating delicious and nutritious meals.

FOOD FOR THOUGHT

Here are a few more notes before you get started! All of the recipes in this book can be mixed and matched to your liking. The best part of making lunches is incorporating things you (or they) love to tailor their meals to their preferences. Most importantly, don't forget to have fun!

At the end of the day, we're just doing our best. Do what you can with the time and money you have! Things can get expensive and overwhelming, so start slow, and you can always add more later! I think of it as a great investment toward becoming a better cook, learning something new, and creating something beautiful and oh so yummy!

My youngest, Olive, is the pickiest out of my three girls. If she could, she would eat ramen noodles and cheese fries every day. She is also allergic to eggs and peanuts. My oldest, Adeline, loves spicy foods and is pretty open to trying new things, but she doesn't like vegetables. My middle child, Maxine, doesn't like trying new things, but she will because she knows I make her meals with love. She ends up liking almost everything, but she's also not big on vegetables. I try to accommodate all their wants and needs and work to make sure they're still eating healthy and trying different things.

COMMUNICATION IS KEY! HAVE THE LUNCH TALK.

Get to know when school lunchtime is. It is important to know when and how long they actually get to eat. On my days off of work, I would visit my kids during their lunches at school. (We were allowed to do so before the pandemic and before security measures became stricter.) That's how I figured out that they get a 30-minute lunch break. In actuality, by the time they line up and make it to the lunch room, about 6 minutes has gone by, and if they are little and struggle to open and close things in their lunch box, that takes another 5 minutes. They eat and talk for about 15 minutes, then it's time to clean up and go out for recess. Lunchtime is really short—even shorter for kids who have to wait in line for school lunch. These days, I just ask their teacher and figure out what's best for them to eat a nutritious lunch quickly and safely.

TIME-SAVING TIP

Unwrap and peel everything you can for them to make lunchtime more efficient! Cutting foods into shapes makes them not only fun to eat but also helps avoid any choking hazards when they are in a rush.

TEST OUT EQUIPMENT

Have your little ones open everything at home first to make sure they can! Most times, teachers and aides at school can't help everyone open their lunches, and by the time they do get to assist them, more precious lunch time has passed.

COMPROMISE

I always encourage my children to give everything a try! You never know what you might end up enjoying if you don't give it a chance. I also like to include treats and snacks as incentives for them to eat the nutritious food first and then indulge in a treat afterward. :)

SEAL WITH A KISS

I love adding personal notes to my daughters' lunches. It brings back fond memories of my own school days when I would exchange decorated notes, often adorned with quotes and song lyrics, with friends. Writing these notes allows me to express my love for my girls and lets them know that I miss them throughout the day.

Over the years, it has become a special way for us to connect on a deeper level. If my daughters are facing challenges or having a tough week, I aim to provide encouragement and support through my words. And when they have tests or important events, I want them to feel my unwavering presence. A simple joke or funny message in the middle of their day holds more significance than one might imagine, and I'm touched to know that my girls have cherished every single note I've written.

Experiment with adding notes to your packed lunches, and make sure to always seal them with a kiss!

KITCHEN TIPS

MEASURES & CONVERSIONS

60 drops = 1 teaspoon (5 ml)

16 dashes = 1 teaspoon (5 ml)

8 pinches = 1 teaspoon (5 ml)

1½ teaspoons = ½ tablespoon (7.5 ml)

3 teaspoons = 1 tablespoon (15 ml)

2 tablespoons = 1 fluid ounce (30 ml)

4 tablespoons = ¼ cup (60 ml)

2⅔ fluid ounces  = ⅓ cup (80 ml)

4 fluid ounces =   ½ cup (120 ml)

8 fluid ounces  = 1 cup (240 ml)

2 cups  = 1 pint (480 ml)

4 cups  = 1 quart (960 ml)

135°F (57°C)
beef (medium rare)
lamb (rare)

150°F (66°C)
beef (medium well)
pork (medium)

165°F (74°C)
chicken & turkey
lamb (well done)

125°F (52°C)
beef (rare)

145°F (63°C)
beef (medium)
lamb & pork (medium rare)
fish & shellfish

160°F (71°C)
beef (well done)
lamb & pork (medium)
ground beef
egg dishes

KNIFE CUTS

CUBE

fine brunoise
1/16-inch (1.5 mm) cube

brunoise (fine dice)
1/8-inch (3 mm) cube

small dice
1/4-inch (6 mm) cube

medium dice
1/2-inch (1 cm) cube

large dice
3/4-inch (2 cm) cube

STRIP

fine julienne
1/16 inch sq. x 2 inches
(1.5 mm x 5 cm)

julienne
1/8 inch sq. x 2 inches
(3 mm x 5 cm)

allumette
1/4 inch sq. x 3 inches
(6 mm x 7.5 cm)

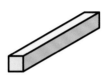

batonnet
1/2 inch sq. x 3 inches
(1 cm x 7.5 cm)

IRREGULAR

mince
1/16 inch
(1.5 mm)

chop
1/8 to 1/4 inch
(3 to 6 mm)

OTHER

rondelle
1/4 inch sq. x 3 inches
(6 mm x 7.5 mm)

chiffonade
rolled and sliced finely

ALLERGEN INFORMATION

In this book, you'll discover a wide array of dishes that cater to various dietary needs, including dairy-free, gluten-free, nut-free, and vegan options. I understand the challenges of navigating food allergies, because Olive (my youngest) has food allergies, so I've included yummy creations that she—and others facing similar challenges—can enjoy without worry.

Next to each recipe in the table of contents (pages 6 and 7), you'll find icons noting which recipes are dairy-free, gluten-free, nut-free, and/or vegan, making it simple to accommodate your specific dietary requirements.

BREAKFAST FOR LUNCH

"Lovefool" – **The Cardigans**

You are stronger
than you think.

I
LOVE
YOU

FRIED CHICKEN SKEWERS + FLUFFY RAINBOW WAFFLES

Get ready to taste the rainbow with these fluffy rainbow waffles and juicy fried chicken skewers. Whipped cream and letter sprinkles make this lunch even more special. Serve alongside crinkle-cut carrots and steamed edamame to complete the meal.

FRIED CHICKEN SKEWERS

15 minutes
Prep time

15 minutes
Cook Time

30 minutes
Total Time

Level: ★★☆☆

Serves 4

1. In a large bowl, whisk together the flour, paprika, garlic powder, onion powder, cayenne, salt, and black pepper.

2. Pour the buttermilk into a wide, shallow bowl.

3. Heat about 3 inches (7.5 cm) of vegetable oil in a large pot or Dutch oven to 350°F (180°C).

4. Dip each piece of chicken into the flour mixture, shaking off any excess.

5. Dip the chicken into the buttermilk, then back into the flour mixture, coating fully each time.

6. Fry the chicken bites in batches until golden brown and crispy, 4 to 6 minutes.

7. Remove the chicken bites with a slotted spoon and place them onto a paper towel–lined plate to drain the excess oil.

8. Skewer them on cute food picks! Serve with homemade ranch or your favorite dip.

INGREDIENTS

1 cup (120 g) all-purpose flour

1 tablespoon paprika

1 tablespoon garlic powder

1 tablespoon onion powder

1 teaspoon cayenne

1 teaspoon kosher salt

½ teaspoon black pepper

1 cup (240 ml) buttermilk

1 pound (454 g) chicken breast, cut into bite-size pieces

Vegetable oil

Homemade Ranch (page 101), for serving

TOOLS

Deep fry thermometer

Skewer sticks

FLUFFY RAINBOW WAFFLES

15 minutes
Prep time

2 to 3 minutes
per waffle
Cook Time

20 to 30 minutes
Total Time

Level: ★★☆☆

Serves 4

INGREDIENTS

2 cups (240 g) all-purpose flour

¼ cup (50 g) sugar

1 tablespoon baking powder

½ teaspoon kosher salt

2 eggs, yolks and whites separated

1¾ cups (420 ml) milk

8 tablespoons unsalted butter, melted and cooled

1 teaspoon vanilla extract

Red, orange, yellow, green, blue, and purple food coloring (see page 19)

Whipped cream and sprinkles, for serving, optional

TOOLS

Waffle iron

Squeeze bottle, optional

---

1. In a large bowl, whisk together the flour, sugar, baking powder, and salt.

2. In a medium bowl, whisk together the egg yolks, milk, butter, vanilla, and 3 tablespoons of water.

3. Add the wet ingredients to the dry ingredients and mix until smooth.

4. Whisk the egg whites until stiff peaks form. Gently fold in the egg whites.

5. Divide the batter among six small bowls and add a few drops of each food coloring to each, creating a rainbow palate. Mix well until the colors are incorporated into the batter. Add to different squeeze bottles, if using.

6. Starting with the purple batter, spoon or squeeze the batter into the center of a waffle iron. Spoon a circle of blue batter outside the purple. Continue to spoon circles of batter around the existing batter with the green, yellow, orange, and red batters.

7. Turn your waffle iron to low to medium heat. Cook the waffle until golden brown, 2 to 3 minutes, or until the red light goes off on the waffle iron.

8. Serve with whipped cream and sprinkles, if desired.

TIP: You can skip the coloring to make regular fluffy waffles. You can also freeze the leftovers and save to eat later! Just reheat in the toaster or air fryer.

"You are my sun, my moon, and all of my stars."
—E.E. CUMMINGS

◀◀ ▶ǁ ▶▶

"Get Up" – **New Jeans**

MINI SCOTCH EGGS + BUTTER MASHED POTATOES

Get ready for a mini feast with these adorable mini Scotch eggs! Each perfectly cooked quail egg is coated in crispy bread crumbs, making these both delicious and adorable. I first learned about Scotch eggs in my world cuisine class in college, and I always crave them! They pair perfectly with buttery mashed potatoes, crunchy veggie chips, and a side of cantaloupe flowers and pomegranate seeds.

MINI SCOTCH EGGS

15 minutes
Prep time

10 minutes
Cook Time

25 minutes
Total Time

Level: ★★☆☆　　　　　　　　**Makes 8**

1. Place the eggs in a small pot of cold water and bring to a boil. Reduce the heat to low and simmer for 2 to 3 minutes. Remove from the heat and transfer the eggs to a bowl of ice water to cool. Peel the eggs and set aside.

2. In a large bowl, combine the sausage, flour, salt, pepper, paprika, and thyme. Mix to combine.

3. Divide the sausage mixture into eight equal portions. Flatten each portion in your palm, then place an egg in the center. Wrap the sausage around each egg until completely covered.

4. Roll the sausage-wrapped eggs in the beaten egg and then the bread crumbs until fully coated.

5. Heat enough oil to submerge the Scotch eggs in a deep pan or fryer over high heat to 350°F (175°C). Carefully place the Scotch eggs into the oil and fry until golden brown and cooked through, 3 to 4 minutes, in batches if necessary.

6. Use a slotted spoon to transfer the eggs to drain on paper towels. Garnish with chives if desired.

7. Serve warm or let cool completely before adding to a lunch.

TIP: When packing anything crispy, you want to let it cool completely before packing so it doesn't get soggy.

INGREDIENTS

8 quail eggs

½ pound (227 g) ground pork sausage

¼ cup (30 g) all-purpose flour

½ teaspoon kosher salt

¼ teaspoon black pepper

¼ teaspoon paprika

¼ teaspoon dried thyme

1 egg, beaten

¼ cup (22 g) bread crumbs

Neutral oil

Chopped chives, for garnish

TOOLS

Deep fryer, optional

Deep fry thermometer

BUTTER MASHED POTATOES

10 minutes
Prep time

20 minutes
Cook Time

30 minutes
Total Time

Level: ★☆☆☆

Serves 4

1. Place the potatoes in a large pot and add enough cold water to cover them by about 1 inch (2.5 cm). Add a generous pinch of salt.

2. Bring the water to a boil over high heat, then reduce the heat to medium and simmer for 15 to 20 minutes, until the potatoes are tender when pierced with a fork.

3. Drain the potatoes in a colander, then return them to the pot.

4. Add the butter and heavy cream, then use a potato masher or a hand mixer to mash the potatoes until they are smooth and creamy. Be careful not to overwork the potatoes, or they may become gummy.

5. Season the mashed potatoes to taste with salt and pepper. Garnish with chives if desired.

6. Transfer to a thermos container to keep warm for lunchtime (see Tip).

TIP: Preheat your thermos or stainless container by adding hot water to the inside, and let sit for at least 15 minutes. Drain the water, then dry with a towel. Fill with your warm foods!

INGREDIENTS

4 large russet potatoes, peeled and roughly chopped

Kosher salt and black pepper

8 tablespoons unsalted butter, cut into eight chunks

¼ cup (60 ml) heavy cream or milk

Chopped chives, for garnish

TOOLS

Colander

Potato masher or hand mixer

APPLE PIE OVERNIGHT OATS + TWISTED BACON

Super easy apple pie overnight oats for lunch are a time saver for busy mornings. Rolled oats are soaked in almond milk and infused with the warming flavors of cinnamon and nutmeg. Pair with crispy twisted bacon, which provides a playful combination of sweet and salty flavors. For snacks, dried apricots and macarons are decadent treats.

APPLE PIE OVERNIGHT OATS

10 minutes
Prep time

4 hours
Cook Time

4 hours and 10 minutes
Total Time

Level: ★☆☆☆

Serves 2

INGREDIENTS

1 cup (80 g) rolled oats

1 cup (240 ml) Almond Milk (page 258)

½ cup (120 ml) Homemade Applesauce (page 51)

1 teaspoon vanilla extract

½ teaspoon ground cinnamon

¼ teaspoon ground nutmeg

1 small green apple, diced

1 tablespoon maple syrup, optional

1. In a large bowl, combine the oats, almond milk, applesauce, vanilla, cinnamon, and nutmeg.

2. Divide the mixture into two jars. Add the diced apple on top, then drizzle with maple syrup, if desired.

3. Cover the jars with lids. Transfer to the refrigerator and chill for at least 4 hours or overnight.

4. When you're ready to eat, give the oats a good stir and enjoy!

TWISTED BACON

10 minutes
Prep time

30 minutes
Cook Time

40 minutes
Total Time

Level: ★★☆☆

Serves 4

INGREDIENTS

1 pound (454 g) thin-sliced bacon

2 tablespoons light brown sugar

1 teaspoon black pepper

TOOLS

Skewers

Baking sheets

Aluminum foil or parchment paper

1. Preheat the oven to 350°F (180°C). Line two baking sheets with foil.

2. Lay the bacon on one baking sheet; sprinkle with brown sugar and black pepper.

3. Poke a skewer through each end of a bacon strip. Twist the strip several times around the skewer to make a tight spiral. Return the bacon to the baking sheet.

4. Bake for 20 to 25 minutes, until crispy.

5. Transfer the skewers onto the other baking sheet to cool.

6. Gently remove the skewers and enjoy!

"The Good Part" — **AJR**

"You are beautiful.
You are strong.
You are worth it.
You are loved."

—MACAILE HUTT

FIG & BRIE UPSIDE-DOWN PUFF PASTRY + MANGO CHIA SEED PUDDING

Experience a symphony of flavors with this fig and brie upside-down puff pastry, complemented by a refreshing mango chia seed pudding and a delightful presentation of cauliflower, peppers, and snap peas. Add some cotton candy for a sweet treat.

FIG & BRIE UPSIDE-DOWN PUFF PASTRY

15 minutes
Prep time

20 minutes
Cook Time

35 minutes
Total Time

Level: ★★☆☆	Serves 4

INGREDIENTS

All-purpose flour, for dusting

1 sheet puff pastry, thawed

2 tablespoons honey

4 to 6 fresh figs, sliced

5 to 6 thin slices brie

1 egg, beaten

Fresh thyme or rosemary leaves, optional

TOOLS

Rolling pin

Parchment paper

Baking sheet

1. Preheat the oven to 400°F (200°C). Line a baking sheet with parchment paper.

2. On a lightly floured surface, roll out the puff pastry into a rectangular shape, about ¼-inch (6 mm) thick. Cut into 4-inch (10 cm) long rectangles.

3. Drizzle ½ tablespoon of honey on the parchment paper.

4. Place two to three fig slices overlapping each other, onto the top of the honey. Arrange one to two brie slices on top.

5. Carefully lay a puff pastry rectangle over the figs and brie, pressing the puff pastry sides down onto the parchment paper and creating a border about ½ inch (1 cm) around the filling.

6. Repeat steps 3 through 5 with the remaining honey, figs, brie, and pastry.

7. Lightly brush the tops of the pastry with the beaten egg.

8. Bake for 18 to 20 minutes, until the pastry is golden brown and puffed up.

9. Remove from the oven and let cool for a few minutes, then carefully flip.

10. Garnish with fresh thyme or rosemary leaves, if desired.

NOTE: This works great with other fruits, such as apricots, apples, and pears.

MANGO CHIA SEED PUDDING

15 minutes
Prep time

4 hours
Chill Time

4 hours and 15 minutes
Total Time

Level: ★☆☆☆

Serves 2

1. Place the mango in a blender and blend until smooth. Transfer to a medium bowl.

2. Add the milk, chia seeds, and sweetener, if desired. Mix well.

3. Cover the bowl and refrigerate for at least 4 hours or overnight to allow the chia seeds to absorb the liquid and thicken the pudding.

4. Stir the pudding mixture after a few hours to ensure that the chia seeds are evenly distributed.

5. Once the pudding has thickened to your desired consistency, serve in individual bowls or jars.

6. Top with fresh fruits, such as sliced mangoes or berries.

TIP: Pre-chill your thermos or stainless steel containers to keep things cool by adding ice and water to the container for at least 15 minutes. Drain the water and dry off with a towel, then add your cold food items.

×

INGREDIENTS

1 ripe mango, peeled and diced

1 cup (240 ml) milk

¼ cup (60 ml) chia seeds

1 to 2 tablespoons honey or maple syrup, optional

Fresh fruit, for serving

TOOLS

Blender

"The World is New" — **Save Ferris**

CHORIZO, EGG & CHEESE HOT POCKETS + BREAKFAST POTATOES

This hot pocket is the perfect lunchtime treat. Bite into the warm and flaky pastry, filled with a savory mix of spicy chorizo, scrambled eggs, and gooey cheese. Serve with crispy, seasoned breakfast potatoes that add a satisfying crunch to each bite. Add crisp snap peas and cute gummy bears on the side.

I love you not only for what you are, but for what I am when I am with you.

CHORIZO, EGG & CHEESE HOT POCKETS

15 minutes	35 minutes	50 minutes
Prep time	Cook Time	Total Time

Level: ★★☆☆ **Makes 2**

1. Preheat your oven to 400°F (200°C). Line a baking sheet with parchment paper.

2. Cook the chorizo in a small skillet over medium-high heat until browned and cooked through, 5 to 7 minutes. Remove from the heat and let cool.

3. In a small bowl, whisk the eggs and season with salt and pepper. Cook in the same skillet until set, 2 to 3 minutes, stirring occasionally. Remove from the heat and let cool.

4. Dust a work surface with flour, then roll out the puff pastry and cut it into four equal rectangles.

5. Spoon about 2 tablespoons each of chorizo and scrambled eggs onto two of the squares, leaving a small border around the edges. Sprinkle the cheese on top.

6. Add the remaining puff pastry squares on top and crimp the edges with a fork to seal.

7. Cut a few small slits, or use a cute shape cutter on the top of each pocket to allow steam to escape while baking.

8. Brush the tops with the egg wash.

9. Transfer the pockets to the baking sheet and bake for 13 to 15 minutes, until golden brown.

10. Top with Italian seasoning, if desired. Serve hot or let cool completely before adding to your lunch box.

INGREDIENTS

½ pound (227 g) ground chorizo

4 eggs

Kosher salt and black pepper

All-purpose flour, for dusting

1 sheet thawed puff pastry

1 cup (113 g) shredded cheddar

1 egg, beaten

Italian seasoning, optional

TOOLS

Parchment paper

Baking sheet

Rolling pin

Food shape cutter, optional

Pastry brush

BREAKFAST POTATOES

15 minutes
Prep time

25 minutes
Cook Time

40 minutes
Total Time

Level: ★☆☆☆   **Serves 4 to 6**

1. Heat the olive oil in a large skillet over medium-high heat. Add the onion and sauté until translucent, 8 to 10 minutes.

2. Add the bell peppers and garlic and cook until they start to soften, 2 to 3 minutes.

3. Add the potatoes and stir to combine. Season with salt and pepper to taste and mix well.

4. Cover the skillet and allow the potatoes to cook until golden brown and crispy, 12 to 15 minutes, stirring occasionally.

5. Serve hot or let cool completely before adding to your lunch!

SPECIAL TOUCHES: Cut your bell peppers into cute shapes to make them more appealing.

INGREDIENTS

2 tablespoons olive oil

1 large onion, diced

1 red bell pepper, diced

1 green bell pepper, diced

2 to 3 garlic cloves, minced

4 medium russet potatoes, peeled and diced

Kosher salt and black pepper

FLUFFY EGG BITES + HOMEMADE APPLESAUCE

For a quick and flavorful lunch, combine bacon-and-cheese egg bites with smooth, homemade applesauce. Serve with sliced heart-shaped strawberries and chocolate-covered pretzels for a sweet treat.

FLUFFY EGG BITES

10 minutes	25 minutes	35 minutes
Prep time	Cook Time	Total Time

Level: ★☆☆☆ **Makes 6**

INGREDIENTS

2 slices bacon

Nonstick cooking spray

4 large eggs

¼ cup (60 ml) milk

Kosher salt and black
  pepper

¼ cup (28 g) shredded
  cheddar

TOOLS

6-cup muffin pan

1. Heat a medium nonstick skillet over medium heat. Cook the bacon until crispy, 4 to 5 minutes on each side. Cool and chop into small pieces.

2. Preheat the oven to 375°F (190°C). Spray a muffin pan with nonstick cooking spray.

3. In a medium bowl, beat the eggs until they are light and frothy. Add the milk, and a pinch of salt and pepper. Mix well, then stir in the cheddar and bacon.

4. Pour the egg mixture into the muffin cups, filling them about three-fourths of the way full.

5. Bake for 20 to 25 minutes, until the egg bites are golden brown and fluffy.

6. Remove from the oven and let cool for a few minutes before serving.

HOMEMADE APPLESAUCE

10 minutes	20 minutes	30 minutes
Prep time	Cook Time	Total Time

Level: ★☆☆☆ **Makes 1½ to 2 cups** (360 to 480 ml)

INGREDIENTS

6 to 8 medium apples, peeled, cored, and chopped (I like McIntosh and Golden Delicious)

2 tablespoons honey or maple syrup

1 teaspoon ground cinnamon

TOOLS

Blender

1. To a large saucepan, add the apples and ½ cup (120 ml) water. Bring to a boil.

2. Add honey for sweetness and cinnamon for flavor. Reduce the heat to low and let the apples simmer for about 25 minutes, stirring occasionally, until soft and tender. Remove from the heat and let cool for a few minutes.

3. Transfer to a blender and puree the cooked apples until smooth.

4. Mix well and serve warm or chilled.

"Be a voice, not an echo."

—ALBERT EINSTEIN

◀◀ ▶❚❚ ▶▶

"Dreams" — **Fleetwood Mac**

MINI BREAKFAST BURRITOS + PICO DE GALLO

Mini breakfast burritos are quick to make and packed with goodness. These little bundles of joy are filled with scrambled eggs, crispy bacon, potatoes, and cheese. Serve with pico de gallo, guacamole, and a dollop of sour cream. For a refreshing treat, add a side of crisp cucumbers sprinkled with Tajín.

MINI BREAKFAST BURRITOS

10 minutes
Prep time

20 minutes
Cook Time

30 minutes
Total Time

Level: ★☆☆☆	Makes 2

1. Preheat the oven to 350°F (180°C).

2. Heat a medium skillet over medium-high heat and add the potato cubes. Cook until golden brown and crispy, stirring occasionally, 8 to 10 minutes. Remove from the skillet and set aside.

3. In the same skillet, cook the bacon until crispy, 2 to 3 minutes on each side. Remove from the skillet and let cool, then chop into small pieces.

4. Crack the eggs into a bowl and whisk with a pinch of salt and pepper.

5. Pour the eggs into the skillet and cook over medium heat, stirring occasionally, until scrambled and cooked through, about 3 minutes.

6. Warm the tortillas in the microwave for a few seconds until soft and pliable.

7. Divide the eggs, potatoes, bacon, and cheese evenly between the two tortillas.

8. Fold the bottom of one tortilla up over the fillings and then fold in both sides tightly. Roll to make a burrito. Repeat with the second tortilla.

9. Place the burritos on a baking sheet and bake for 5 to 7 minutes, until the cheese is melted and the tortillas are golden brown.

10. Remove from the oven, let cool for a few minutes, and serve.

INGREDIENTS

1 medium russet potato, peeled and diced

2 slices bacon

3 eggs

Kosher salt and black pepper

2 small flour tortillas

¼ cup (28 g) shredded cheddar

TOOLS

Baking sheet

PICO DE GALLO

15 minutes
Prep time

1 hour
Chill Time

1 hour and 15 minutes
Total Time

Level: ★☆☆☆

Serves 4

1. Combine the tomatoes, onion, cilantro, jalapeño, and garlic in a large bowl and stir well to combine.

2. Add the sugar, and salt and pepper to taste. Squeeze lime juice over the mixture and stir it in.

3. Cover the bowl with plastic wrap and refrigerate for at least 1 hour before serving.

✕

INGREDIENTS

4 medium ripe tomatoes, diced

½ red onion, finely chopped

⅓ cup (20 g) finely chopped fresh cilantro leaves

1 jalapeño, seeded and finely chopped

2 garlic cloves, minced

1 teaspoon sugar

Kosher salt and black pepper

Juice of 1 lime

SUGAR & SPICE BACON JAM + MINI EVERYTHING BAGELS

I present to you a delectable bacon jam served with mini everything bagels. The jam is sweet and salty, and the bagels are so easy to make. Together, they are the perfect combo. I include snap pea crisps on the side for some crunch!

SUGAR & SPICE BACON JAM

10 minutes
Prep time

40 minutes
Cook Time

50 minutes
Total Time

Level: ★☆☆☆

Makes 1 to ½ cups
(200 to 300 g)

INGREDIENTS

½ pound (227 g) bacon, chopped

½ large onion, diced

2 garlic cloves, minced

¼ cup (36 g) brown sugar

2 tablespoons apple cider vinegar

2 tablespoons maple syrup

⅛ teaspoon black pepper

⅛ teaspoon smoked paprika

1. In a large skillet or pot over medium heat, cook the bacon until crispy, 5 to 8 minutes.

2. Remove the bacon from the pan with a slotted spoon and place it on a paper towel–lined plate to drain. Leave about 2 tablespoons of bacon grease in the skillet and discard the rest.

3. Add the onion to the skillet and sauté until golden brown, stirring occasionally, 3 to 5 minutes. Add the garlic and sauté until lightly golden, 1 more minute.

4. Reduce the heat to low and add the cooked bacon back to the skillet. Add the brown sugar, vinegar, maple syrup, pepper, and paprika and stir well to combine.

5. Simmer over low heat for 20 to 30 minutes, stirring occasionally, until the mixture thickens and becomes jam-like. Remove from the heat and let cool for a few minutes.

6. Serve warm or at room temperature.

MINI EVERYTHING BAGELS

15 minutes
Prep time

25 minutes
Cook Time

40 minutes
Total Time

Level: ★☆☆☆

Makes 6

INGREDIENTS

1 cup (120 g) all-purpose flour, plus more for dusting

¾ cup (180 g) plain Greek yogurt

1 teaspoon baking powder

1 tablespoon everything bagel seasoning

TOOLS

Baking sheet

Parchment paper

Wire rack

1. Preheat your oven to 350°F (180°C). Line a baking sheet with parchment paper.

2. In a medium bowl, combine the flour, yogurt, and baking powder. Using your hands, mix well until a dough forms.

3. Dust a clean surface with flour and transfer the dough onto it. Knead the dough with your hands for a few minutes until it becomes smooth and elastic.

4. Divide the dough into six equal portions. Roll each portion into a ball, then flatten it slightly and use your finger to poke a hole in the middle, making six mini bagels.

5. Place the bagels onto the baking sheet. Sprinkle the everything bagel seasoning evenly over the tops of the bagels.

6. Bake for 22 to 25 minutes, until the bagels are golden brown and slightly crispy.

7. Remove from the oven and let cool on a wire rack before serving.

"First Time (feat. Dylan Matthew)" — **Seven Lions, SLANDER & Dabin**

Be proud of who you are and not ashamed of how someone else sees you.

ORANGE SWEET ROLLS + MINI GREEN JUICE

These delicious rolls are a delightful twist on the classic cinnamon roll, infused with bright and zesty orange flavor. Make a refreshing mini green juice to drink on the side, then serve with a salami rose and a vibrant assortment of broccoli and juicy blackberries.

ORANGE SWEET ROLLS

30 minutes
Prep time

30 minutes
Cook Time

2½ hours
with rising time
Total Time

Level: ★★★☆

Makes 12

1. Make the dough: In the bowl of a stand mixer fitted with the paddle attachment, combine 2 cups (240 g) of the flour, sugar, yeast, and salt.

2. In a microwave-safe bowl, microwave the milk and butter in 15 to 30 second intervals until the mixture is warm (not hot) and the butter is mostly melted. Add to the flour mixture.

3. Add the egg. Beat on low, gradually increasing to high until combined, 2 minutes. Add 1 cup (120 g) of flour, reducing the speed of the mixer as you add, beating until combined.

4. Gradually add the remaining 2 cups (240 g) of flour, until the dough is shaggy and starts to pull away from the bowl.

5. Change to the dough hook and knead until the dough becomes lightly shiny and forms a smooth ball, about 5 minutes.

6. Transfer the dough to a large greased bowl and cover. Let rise in a warm place for 1 hour or until doubled in size.

7. Meanwhile, make the filling: In a small bowl, use a fork to combine the butter, sugar, and orange zest. Mix until fluffy.

8. Punch the dough down and use a lightly floured rolling pin to roll it out onto a lightly floured surface into a horizontal rectangular shape, 12 x 18 inches (30 x 45 cm).

9. Spread the filling mixture evenly over the dough.

10. Roll up the dough tightly, starting from the long side closest to you. Cut the roll into 12 even pieces.

11. Place the rolls in a lightly greased 9 x 13-inch (23 x 33 cm) baking dish, cover with a clean kitchen towel, and let rise for about 30 minutes.

12. Meanwhile, preheat the oven to 350°F (180°C). Bake the rolls for 25 to 30 minutes, until golden brown.

13. While the rolls are baking, make the glaze. In a small bowl, whisk together the powdered sugar, orange juice, and heavy cream until smooth.

14. Drizzle the glaze over the warm rolls and serve.

INGREDIENTS

DOUGH
5 cups (600 g) all-purpose flour, divided, plus more for dusting

⅓ cup (67 g) granulated sugar

One ¼-ounce (7 g) packet rapid rise instant yeast (2¼ teaspoons)

1 teaspoon kosher salt

1½ cups (360 g) whole milk

6 tablespoons unsalted butter, cubed, plus more for greasing

1 egg, at room temperature

FILLING
8 tablespoons unsalted butter, softened

⅔ cup (133 g) granulated sugar

Finely grated zest of 2 oranges

GLAZE
1 cup (120 g) powdered sugar

3 tablespoons freshly squeezed orange juice

1 tablespoon heavy cream

TOOLS
Stand mixer

Rolling pin

Baking dish (9 x 13 inches / 23 x 33 cm)

MINI GREEN JUICE

10 minutes	0 minutes	10 minutes
Prep time	Cook Time	Total Time

Level: ★☆☆☆   **Makes 6**

1. Place the banana, spinach, kale, pineapple, coconut water, and lemon juice in a blender.

2. Blend until smooth. If the mixture is too thick, add a little more liquid. For a smoother consistency, strain through a cheesecloth.

3. Taste and adjust the sweetness, if desired, by adding a small amount of honey or maple syrup.

4. Pour the green juice into mini bottles or small serving glasses.

NOTE: Mix up the flavors in this juice by adding other fruits, such as apples or berries.

INGREDIENTS

1 ripe banana, sliced

1 cup (30 g) lightly packed spinach leaves

½ cup (15 g) lightly packed kale leaves

½ cup (80 g) ½-inch (1 cm) pineapple chunks

½ cup (120 ml) coconut water or water

1 tablespoon fresh lemon juice

Honey or maple syrup, optional

TOOLS

Blender or juicer

Cheesecloth, optional

Six 2-ounce (59 ml) bottles

HEART-SHAPED POTATO CROQUETTES + SAUTÉED BUTTER MUSHROOMS

These heart-shaped potato croquettes are crispy on the outside and soft and creamy on the inside. Pair them with sautéed butter mushrooms for a savory and earthy flavor. Enjoy the crunch of carrot chips and refreshing cucumber slices. Juicy cherry tomatoes, dried pineapples, and confetti cookies are a colorful treat. Don't forget to add in a side of ketchup for the croquettes!

HEART-SHAPED POTATO CROQUETTES

15 minutes
Prep time

30 minutes
Cook Time

45 minutes
Total Time

Level: ★★★☆

Makes 12

INGREDIENTS

4 medium potatoes, peeled and chopped

Kosher salt and black pepper

½ cup (45 g) grated Parmesan

¼ cup (15 g) chopped fresh parsley

¼ cup (30 g) all-purpose flour

2 eggs, beaten

1 cup (90 g) bread crumbs

Neutral oil, for frying

Kewpie mayonnaise and ketchup, for serving

TOOLS

Potato masher

Baking sheet

Heart-shaped cookie cutter, optional

1. Boil the potatoes in a pot of salted water for about 15 minutes, until tender.

2. Drain the potatoes and mash them thoroughly with a potato masher. Add salt, pepper, Parmesan, and parsley. Mix well.

3. Spread the potato mixture onto a baking sheet and let cool in the refrigerator for about 30 minutes.

4. Remove from the refrigerator, then use a heart-shaped cookie cutter to cut out 12 croquettes. If you don't have one, you can mold the croquettes into heart shapes.

5. Roll each croquette in flour, dip it in beaten egg, and coat it in bread crumbs.

6. Heat about 1 inch (2.5 cm) of oil in a large pan over medium heat. Fry the croquettes until golden brown, 3 to 4 minutes on each side.

7. Transfer the croquettes to paper towels to drain.

8. Serve hot with kewpie mayo and ketchup or your favorite dipping sauce. Cool completely before adding to your lunch!

SAUTÉED BUTTER MUSHROOMS

5 minutes
Prep time

15 minutes
Cook Time

20 minutes
Total Time

Level: ★☆☆☆

Serves 4

INGREDIENTS

2 tablespoons butter or olive oil

1 pound (450 g) mushrooms (such as button or cremini), sliced

2 garlic cloves, minced

Kosher salt and black pepper

Fresh parsley or thyme leaves, optional

1. Melt the butter in a large skillet over medium heat. Add the mushrooms and sauté until they start to brown and release their moisture, 5 to 7 minutes, stirring occasionally.

2. Add the garlic and cook until fragrant, 1 to 2 minutes. Season with salt and pepper to taste.

3. Cook until the mushrooms are cooked to your desired tenderness, 2 to 3 more minutes.

4. Remove from the heat and garnish with fresh parsley or thyme leaves, if desired.

Dream big, work hard, stay focused, and surround yourself with good people.

◀◀ ▶ǁ ▶▶

"Sunroof" — **Nicky Youre and Dazy**

CRUNCHY NUT GRANOLA + CARAMELIZED BANANA BREAD

This breakfast for lunch features crunchy granola and banana bread served with a delightful side of creamy Greek yogurt and a medley of mixed berries. The granola is high in fiber, protein, and healthy fats to keep you fueled throughout the day. It pairs perfectly with the caramelized banana bread, a fun twist on the classic.

CRUNCHY NUT GRANOLA

10 minutes
Prep time

25 minutes
Cook Time

35 minutes
Total Time

Level: ★☆☆☆	Makes 5 cups (575 g)

1. Preheat your oven to 350°F (180°C). Line a rimmed baking sheet with parchment paper.

2. In a large bowl, combine the oats, nuts, and seeds. Stir until well combined.

3. In a small saucepan, combine the honey, coconut oil, vanilla, cinnamon, and salt. Heat over low heat until the oil has melted and the mixture is smooth, about 2 minutes.

4. Pour the liquid mixture over the oat mixture, and stir until everything is evenly coated.

5. Spread the granola mixture in an even layer on the baking sheet.

6. Bake for 20 to 25 minutes, stirring halfway through, until the granola is golden brown and crispy.

7. Remove from the oven and let cool completely before storing in an airtight container for up to 6 weeks.

INGREDIENTS

3 cups (295 g) old-fashioned rolled oats

1 cup (120 g) nuts, such as almonds, pecans, and walnuts

½ cup (70 g) seeds, such as pumpkin, sunflower, and chia

¼ cup (60 ml) honey or maple syrup

¼ cup (60 ml) solid coconut oil

1 teaspoon vanilla extract

1 teaspoon ground cinnamon

¼ teaspoon kosher salt

TOOLS

Parchment paper

Baking sheet

CARAMELIZED BANANA BREAD

15 minutes
Prep time

55 minutes
Cook Time

2 ½ hours
with cooling time
Total Time

| Level: ★★★☆ | Makes 1 |

1. Preheat your oven to 350°F (180°C). Grease a loaf pan with butter.

2. In a medium bowl, whisk together the flour, baking soda, cinnamon, and salt.

3. In a large bowl, mix the bananas, butter, brown sugar, egg, and vanilla.

4. Add the dry ingredients to the wet mixture and mix until well incorporated.

5. Pour the batter into the loaf pan and set aside.

6. Make the caramelized bananas: To a nonstick frying pan over medium heat, add the sliced bananas and sprinkle sugar on top. Stir occasionally until the bananas are caramelized, 2 to 3 minutes.

7. Place the caramelized bananas on top of the batter in the pan.

8. Bake for 40 to 50 minutes, until a toothpick comes out clean. Remove from the oven and let cool for 10 minutes before slicing and serving.

INGREDIENTS

8 tablespoons unsalted butter, melted, plus more for greasing

1½ cups (180 g) all-purpose flour

1 teaspoon baking soda

½ teaspoon ground cinnamon

½ teaspoon kosher salt

3 ripe bananas, mashed

½ cup (100 g) packed light brown sugar

1 large egg, at room temperature

1 teaspoon vanilla extract

CARAMELIZED BANANAS

1 ripe but firm banana, halved lengthwise

2 tablespoons sugar

TOOLS

Loaf pan (8½ x 4½ x 2½ inches / 21 x 11 x 6 cm)

MOCHI DONUT BALLS WITH SWEET CREAM GLAZE

These donuts are soft, chewy, and coated in a creamy and sweet glaze. Each bite is a delicious combination of sweet flavor and melt-in-your-mouth texture, making these donuts perfect for breakfast or dessert.

MOCHI DONUT BALLS WITH SWEET CREAM GLAZE

20 minutes
Prep time

10 minutes
Cook Time

30 minutes
Total Time

Level: ★★★☆

Makes 12

INGREDIENTS

1 cup (132 g) glutinous rice flour (I like Erawan brand)

2 tablespoons all-purpose flour

½ teaspoon baking soda

2 tablespoons granulated sugar

1 tablespoon softened butter

¼ teaspoon kosher salt

½ cup (120 ml) hot water

Canola or vegetable oil, for frying

SWEET CREAM GLAZE

1 cup (120 g) powdered sugar

2 tablespoons heavy cream

½ teaspoon vanilla extract

TOOLS

Deep fryer, optional

Deep fry thermometer

Slotted spoon

1. In a large bowl, combine the glutinous rice flour, all-purpose flour, baking soda, granulated sugar, butter, and salt.

2. Slowly add the hot water, 1 tablespoon at a time, stirring and mixing as you go, until incorporated.

3. Use your hands to knead the dough, 2 to 3 minutes. The mixture should be soft.

4. Take about 1 tablespoon of dough and form into a 1-inch (2.5 cm) ball. Repeat with the remaining dough.

5. Heat enough oil to submerge the donuts in a deep fryer or skillet over medium-high heat (340°F/170°C).

6. Carefully drop in the balls, making sure to not overcrowd the skillet. Fry the donuts until golden brown on the outside and cooked through, 3 to 5 minutes. Stir frequently.

7. Use a slotted spoon to remove the donuts from the oil and place them on a paper towel–lined plate to cool.

8. Meanwhile, make the glaze. In a small bowl, whisk together the powdered sugar, heavy cream, and vanilla until smooth and creamy.

9. When the donuts have cooled slightly, dip them into the glaze and transfer to a wire rack to set.

10. Enjoy warm or let cool.

NOTE: You can skip the glaze and roll these donuts in some cinnamon and sugar instead. They are also good with a filling in the middle, such as strawberry jam, Nutella, or sweet red bean. The possibilities are endless!

CREAM CHEESE- STUFFED FRENCH TOAST STICKS + BLUEBERRY COMPOTE + STAR-SHAPED POTATOES

Made with slices of soft bread, a rich cream cheese filling, and a touch of cinnamon sugar, these French toast sticks are heavenly. They pair perfectly with a simple, sweet blueberry compote. For the sides, add in star-shaped potatoes and a bundle of carrot sticks.

You are my favorite hello and my hardest goodbye.

CREAM CHEESE–STUFFED FRENCH TOAST STICKS

15 minutes
Prep time

10 minutes
Cook Time

25 minutes
Total Time

Level: ★★☆☆

Serves 4

1. In a medium bowl, combine the cream cheese, sugar, and vanilla. Stir until smooth.

2. Spread the mixture evenly onto four slices of toasted bread. Top with the remaining four slices to make sandwiches.

3. Cut each sandwich into sticks, about 1-inch (2.5 cm) wide. Remove the crusts, if desired.

4. In a shallow dish, whisk together the eggs, milk, and cinnamon.

5. Heat a large nonstick skillet or griddle over medium heat. Add the butter and let it melt, spreading it evenly across the surface.

6. Dip each toast stick into the egg mixture, allowing it to soak for a few seconds on each side. Shake off any excess liquid and place the sticks onto the hot skillet.

7. Cook until golden brown and crispy, 2 to 3 minutes on each side, working in batches if needed.

8. Transfer the toast sticks to a paper towel–lined plate to absorb any excess grease.

9. Serve warm, dusted with powdered sugar, drizzled with maple syrup, or served with blueberry compote.

✕

INGREDIENTS

4 ounces (113 g) cream cheese, softened

2 tablespoons powdered sugar

1 teaspoon vanilla extract

8 slices of bread (white, whole wheat, or your preferred type), toasted

2 large eggs

½ cup (120 ml) milk

½ teaspoon ground cinnamon

2 tablespoons unsalted butter

FOR SERVING

Powdered sugar

Maple syrup

Blueberry Compote (page 73)

BLUEBERRY COMPOTE

5 minutes
Prep time

20 minutes
Cook Time

25 minutes
Total Time

Level: ★☆☆☆

Makes 2 cups (540 g)

INGREDIENTS

2 cups (340 g) fresh or frozen blueberries

¼ cup (50 g) sugar

1 tablespoon fresh lemon juice

¼ teaspoon ground cinnamon

1. In a medium saucepan over medium-low heat, combine the blueberries, sugar, lemon juice, cinnamon, and ¼ cup (60 ml) water. Stir everything together until the sugar dissolves, 2 to 3 minutes.

2. Bring to a boil, then reduce the heat and simmer for 10 to 15 minutes, stirring occasionally to prevent sticking, until the blueberries have broken down and the mixture has thickened.

3. Remove from heat and let cool slightly. Serve warm or chilled, or store in the refrigerator for up to 2 weeks.

STAR-SHAPED POTATOES

15 minutes
Prep time

30 minutes
Cook Time

30 minutes
Total Time

Level: ★★☆☆

Serves 2 to 4

INGREDIENTS

2 large russet potatoes, peeled and thinly sliced

Vegetable oil

1 teaspoon kosher salt

1 teaspoon black pepper

1 teaspoon garlic powder

1 teaspoon paprika

TOOLS

Star-shaped food cutter

Deep fry thermometer

1. Use a star-shaped food cutter to cut the potatoes into star shapes (see Note). Soak in a bowl of cold water for 15 minutes. Dry completely with a paper towel.

2. In a medium pot, heat 2 inches (5 cm) of oil to 350°F (170°C).

3. Fry the potato stars in small batches until golden brown and crispy, 3 to 4 minutes.

4. Remove the potatoes from the oil and drain on a paper towel–lined plate.

5. Season with salt, pepper, garlic powder, and paprika.

NOTE: I also like to fry up the potato leftovers!

HAM & CHEESE CRÊPES + SAUTÉED SPINACH

Get ready to say "Ooh là là!" with these ham and cheese crêpes! The batter is versatile and easy-to-make, so you can customize these crêpes with your favorite filling, too. Pair with a side of savory sautéed spinach, cute watermelon flowers, and rainbow cereal.

HAM & CHEESE CRÊPES

10 minutes
Prep time

15 minutes
Cook Time

25 minutes
Total Time

Level: ★★☆☆

Makes 8

INGREDIENTS

1 cup (125 g) all-purpose flour

2 eggs

½ cup (120 ml) milk

¼ teaspoon kosher salt

2 tablespoons butter, melted

6 to 8 ounces (200 g) deli ham, thinly sliced

4 ounces (113 g) shredded cheese (such as cheddar or Swiss)

TOOLS

Baking sheet

Aluminum foil or parchment paper

1. Preheat the oven to 375°F (190°C). Line a baking sheet with parchment paper or foil.

2. In a medium bowl, whisk together the flour and eggs.

3. Gradually add the milk and ½ cup (120 ml) water, whisking until the batter is smooth. Whisk in the butter and salt.

4. Heat a medium nonstick skillet over medium-high heat. Pour about ¼ cup (60 ml) of batter onto the skillet and swirl it around to coat the bottom of the skillet.

5. Cook the crêpe until the edges start to turn golden brown, about 2 minutes. Flip the crêpe over and cook on the other side until golden brown, 1 more minute.

6. Repeat with the remaining batter, stacking the cooked crêpes on a plate and covering them with a towel to keep them warm.

7. Place a crêpe on a work surface, then set one slice of ham and a sprinkle of shredded cheese on one half of the crêpe.

8. Fold the other side of the crêpe in half over the filling, then fold the entire crêpe in half to form a triangle. Repeat steps 6 and 7 with the remaining crêpes and filling.

9. Place the crêpes onto the baking sheet. Bake in the oven for 5 minutes, until the cheese is melted and bubbly.

SAUTÉED SPINACH

5 minutes
Prep time

4 minutes
Cook Time

9 minutes
Total Time

Level: ★☆☆☆

Serves 2

INGREDIENTS

1 tablespoon olive oil

2 garlic cloves, minced

1 bunch fresh spinach, tough stems removed

Kosher salt and black pepper

1. In a large skillet, heat the olive oil over medium heat.

2. Add the garlic and cook until fragrant, about 30 seconds, being careful not to burn it.

3. Add the spinach and toss with the garlic and oil until it begins to wilt. Cook, stirring occasionally, until the spinach is fully wilted and cooked through, 3 to 4 minutes.

4. Season with salt and pepper to taste. Remove from the heat and serve immediately.

"Feel Good Inc." — **Gorillaz**

"I hope it's okay
if I love you forever."

—*A STAR IS BORN*

○ ○ ○

SAUSAGE FRENCH TOAST ROLL-UPS + STRAWBERRY DIPPING SAUCE

Dive into a delightful breakfast-for-lunch with these sausage French toast roll-ups. Dip them in a sweet strawberry sauce with some sprinkles on top. Serve with orange slices, adorable strawberry hearts, and a side of veggies. A perfect combination to keep you smiling through your day!

SAUSAGE FRENCH TOAST ROLL-UPS

10 minutes
Prep time

20 minutes
Cook Time

30 minutes
Total Time

Level: ★★☆☆	Makes 8

INGREDIENTS

3 eggs

¼ cup (60 ml) milk

1 teaspoon vanilla extract

½ teaspoon ground cinnamon

Pinch of kosher salt

8 slices white bread

8 pork breakfast sausage links

2 tablespoons unsalted butter

Powdered sugar, for dusting

Maple syrup or honey, for serving, optional

TOOLS

Rolling pin

1. Preheat the oven to 375°F (190°C).

2. In a shallow bowl, whisk the eggs, milk, vanilla, cinnamon, and salt until combined.

3. Using a rolling pin, flatten each slice of bread until it's about ¼-inch (6 mm) thick.

4. Place a sausage link on one end of a slice of bread and roll it up tightly. Repeat with the remaining bread and sausages.

5. Dip the roll-ups in the egg mixture, making sure they are coated well.

6. Heat the butter in an oven-safe skillet over medium heat.

7. Add the roll-ups to the skillet and cook until golden brown, about 2 minutes per side.

8. Place the skillet in the oven and bake for 12 to 15 minutes, until cooked through.

9. Remove from the oven and cool for a few minutes. Remove the toothpicks.

10. Dust with powdered sugar and serve with maple syrup or honey, if desired.

STRAWBERRY DIPPING SAUCE

5 minutes
Prep time

10 minutes
Cook Time

15 minutes
Total Time

Level: ★☆☆☆

Makes 1 cup (240 ml)

1. In a medium saucepan, combine the strawberries, sugar, lemon juice, and ¼ cup (60 ml) water.

2. Cook over medium heat until the strawberries are soft and the liquid has reduced slightly, 8 to 10 minutes.

3. Remove from the heat and let cool for a few minutes.

4. Using a blender or an immersion blender, puree the mixture until smooth. (For a completely smooth sauce, strain the mixture through a fine-mesh strainer.)

5. Serve immediately or store in an airtight container in the refrigerator for up to a week.

✕

INGREDIENTS
1 pound (455 g) fresh strawberries, stemmed

¼ cup (50 g) sugar

2 tablespoons lemon juice

TOOLS
Blender or immersion blender

SANDWICHES, WRAPS & ROLLS

"The best way to predict the future is to create it."
—DENNIS GABOR

◄◄ ▶❚❚ ▶▶

"Island in the Sun" — **Weezer**

EGG SALAD SANDO + PARMESAN ZUCCHINI FRIES

Dive into the deliciousness of an egg salad sandwich paired with crispy Parmesan zucchini fries. To complete the lunch, add juicy grape tomatoes, star-shaped crackers, and refreshing dragon fruit balls. Enjoy!

EGG SALAD SANDO

15 minutes
Prep time

0 minutes
Cook Time

15 minutes
Total Time

Level: ★☆☆☆

Makes 4

1. Place the eggs in a large bowl. Add the mayonnaise, celery, pickles, onion (if using), mustard, salt, and pepper. Gently mix to combine.

2. Place lettuce leaves, if using, on four slices of bread.

3. Spread the egg salad mixture over the lettuce leaves, then top with the other slices of bread.

4. Wrap with plastic wrap or parchment paper and let it set in the refrigerator for 10 minutes.

5. Slice the sandwiches and serve.

TIP: These are great to make ahead! Keep them cool by packing them with an ice pack.

x

INGREDIENTS

6 hard-boiled eggs, peeled and chopped

¼ cup (60 ml) mayonnaise

1 tablespoon finely chopped celery

1 tablespoon chopped dill pickles

1 tablespoon finely chopped red onion, optional

1½ teaspoons Dijon mustard

Kosher salt and black pepper

8 slices milk bread

Lettuce leaves, optional

TOOLS

Plastic wrap or parchment paper

PARMESAN ZUCCHINI FRIES

10 minutes
Prep time

10 minutes
Cook Time

20 minutes
Total Time

Level: ★☆☆☆   **Serves 4**

1. Preheat your air fryer to 400°F (200°C).

2. Cut the zucchini into thin strips, about ½-inch (1cm) thick and 3 inches (7.5 cm) long.

3. In a small bowl, mix the flour, garlic powder, onion powder, salt, and pepper.

4. In another small bowl, beat the eggs.

5. In a third small bowl, mix together the panko and Parmesan.

6. Take a zucchini strip and dip it first in the flour mixture, then in the beaten eggs, and finally in the panko mixture, ensuring that it is well coated. Repeat with the remaining zucchini.

7. Place the zucchini strips in a single layer in the air fryer basket, leaving some space between them. Spray them with cooking spray to help them brown evenly.

8. Cook the strips, flipping halfway through, until golden brown and crispy, 8 to 10 minutes.

9. Serve hot with your favorite dipping sauce, such as marinara or ranch. Cool completely before packing for lunch!

INGREDIENTS

2 medium zucchini

¼ cup (30 g) all-purpose flour

¼ teaspoon garlic powder

¼ teaspoon onion powder

¼ teaspoon kosher salt

⅛ teaspoon black pepper

2 eggs

1 cup (100 g) panko bread crumbs

½ cup (45 g) Parmesan

Nonstick cooking spray

Marinara sauce or ranch dressing, for dipping

TOOLS

Air fryer

I love you for all that you are, all that you have been, and all that you will be.

"Blackbird" — The Beatles

WALDORF CHICKEN SALAD CROISSANT SANDWICH + SMILEY POTATOES + EASY FRY SAUCE

Treat yourself to the ultimate sandwich, featuring a medley of juicy chicken, crunchy walnuts, and tangy grapes, all nestled in a buttery croissant. Serve with adorable potatoes that will bring a smile to anyone's face and an easy fry sauce for dipping all your goodies into.

WALDORF CHICKEN SALAD CROISSANT SANDWICH

10 minutes
Prep time

15 minutes
Cook Time

25 minutes
Total Time

Level: ★☆☆☆

Makes 4

1. Season the chicken with salt and pepper.

2. Heat a large skillet over medium-high heat and add the olive oil. Add the chicken and cook until golden brown and cooked through, 7 to 8 minutes per side. Remove the chicken from the skillet and cut into bite-size pieces.

3. In a large bowl, combine the chicken, grapes, celery, and walnuts.

4. Add mayonnaise and stir to coat. Season with salt and pepper to taste.

5. Halve each croissant lengthwise, then add a few lettuce leaves to each bottom half. Add the chicken salad evenly on top of the lettuce. Top with the other half of the croissant and gently press down.

6. Serve immediately or refrigerate until ready to serve.

INGREDIENTS

2 chicken breasts

Kosher salt and black pepper

1 tablespoon olive oil

1 cup (155 g) seedless red grapes, sliced

½ cup (60 g) sliced celery

3 tablespoons roughly chopped walnuts

½ cup (120 ml) mayonnaise

Butter lettuce leaves

4 croissants

SMILEY POTATOES

30 minutes
Prep time

25 minutes
Cook Time

55 minutes
Total Time

Level: ★★★☆

Makes 24

INGREDIENTS	**TOOLS**
2 large Yukon Gold potatoes, peeled and halved	Parchment paper
	Rolling pin
¾ cup (95 g) cornstarch	Two-inch (5 cm) circle cookie cutter
Kosher salt	Straw
Neutral oil, for frying	Baking sheet
	Wax paper
	½ teaspoon

1. Place the potatoes in a large pot and cover with cold water. Boil until soft and tender, 15 to 20 minutes. Remove from the heat and let cool.

2. Transfer the potatoes to a large bowl and mash. Add the cornstarch and salt to taste. Mix well to form a smooth dough.

3. Transfer to a surface lined with parchment paper and using a rolling pin, roll out the dough until it's 1 inch (2.5 cm) thick.

4. Line a baking sheet with wax paper. Press the cookie cutter into the dough, then transfer the cut-outs to the baking sheet.

5. To make a smiley face on each potato, use a straw to poke out the eyes and a ½ teaspoon to cut out the mouth.

6. Place the baking sheet in the freezer for at least 30 minutes.

7. Heat 1 inch (2.5 cm) of oil in a large pot. Add the potatoes and deep fry until golden brown, 5 to 6 minutes.

8. Remove the potatoes with a slotted spoon and drain off the excess oil on a paper towel.

9. Serve hot. When packing for lunch, let cool completely to keep them crispy!

EASY FRY SAUCE

5 minutes
Prep time

0 minutes
Cook Time

5 minutes
Total Time

Level: ★☆☆☆

Makes 1 cup (240 ml)

INGREDIENTS	
½ cup (120 ml) mayonnaise	1 teaspoon Worcestershire sauce
2 tablespoons ketchup	½ teaspoon garlic powder
1 tablespoon pickle relish	Kosher salt and black pepper

1. In a small bowl, combine the mayonnaise, ketchup, relish, Worcestershire sauce, garlic powder, salt, and pepper.

2. Transfer the fry sauce to a serving dish or individual dipping bowls.

3. Serve with smiley potatoes or any other fried foods.

4. Store in an airtight container in the fridge for up to 1 week.

PEPPERONI & MUSHROOM PIZZA ROLL-UPS + MINI CAPRESE BITES

These roll-ups are so easy and fun to make, and you can switch it up and use any of your favorite toppings. Pair them with mini caprese bites, which I made in my first viral lunch video. Add pretzels, cantaloupe stars, and unicorn cookies on the side to add a touch of magic to this lunch.

PEPPERONI & MUSHROOM PIZZA ROLL-UPS

10 minutes
Prep time

15 minutes
Cook Time

25 minutes
Total Time

Level: ★☆☆☆

Makes 8

INGREDIENTS

½ cup (120 ml) pizza sauce

2 flour tortillas

½ cup (50 g) thinly sliced button mushrooms

½ cup (70 g) sliced pepperoni

¼ cup (25 g) shredded mozzarella

TOOLS

Baking sheet

Parchment paper

1. Preheat the oven to 375°F (190°C). Line a baking sheet with parchment paper.

2. Spread a thin layer of pizza sauce onto each tortilla, then add the mushrooms and pepperoni over the sauce. Sprinkle on the mozzarella.

3. Starting from the bottom, tightly roll up the tortillas to form roll-ups.

4. Place the roll-ups, seam side down, onto the baking sheet.

6. Bake for 3 to 5 minutes, until the cheese is melted.

7. Let cool for a few minutes before serving.

MINI CAPRESE BITES

10 minutes
Prep time

0 minutes
Cook Time

10 minutes
Total Time

Level: ★☆☆☆

Makes 12

INGREDIENTS

12 fresh basil leaves

12 mini mozzarella balls

12 cherry tomatoes

2 to 3 tablespoons balsamic glaze

2 to 3 tablespoons olive oil

Kosher salt and black pepper

TOOLS

12 mini skewers or toothpicks

1. Place a basil leaf, a mozzarella ball, and a tomato onto each skewer.

2. Drizzle with balsamic glaze and olive oil, then season with salt and pepper to taste.

3. Serve immediately and enjoy!

TIP: You can easily make your own balsamic glaze by simmering balsamic vinegar in a small pan for a few minutes until it reaches your desired consistency.

◀◀ ▶❙❙ ▶▶

"Perfect" — **Ed Sheeran**

The greatest gift you can give someone is your time, your attention, and your love.

BBQ PORK SANDWICHES + TANGY COLESLAW + POTATO SALAD

I love a good BBQ, and this pulled pork sandwich recipe is one of Maxine's favorites! The slow-cooked pork is tender and juicy, coated in a sweet and smoky BBQ sauce. This sandwich is perfectly balanced with a crunchy slaw and creamy potato salad. Chili-lime rolled tortilla chips and potato chips complete your meal.

BBQ PORK SANDWICHES

15 minutes
Prep time

4 hours
Cook Time

4 hours and 15 minutes
Total Time

Level: ★★★☆

Makes 4 to 6

1. Preheat the oven to 325°F (165°C).

2. Season the pork shoulder with salt and pepper.

3. Heat a medium skillet over medium-high heat and add about 1 tablespoon of oil. Sear the pork shoulder until golden brown all over, about 10 minutes, reducing the heat as necessary to avoid scorching. Transfer to a snug baking dish.

4. In the same skillet, sauté the onion and garlic until fragrant, about 2 minutes, then add the broth and stir to scrape up any brown bits from the bottom of the skillet.

5. Add the BBQ sauce to the skillet and bring to a simmer.

6. Pour the BBQ sauce mixture over the pork shoulder and cover tightly with foil.

7. Bake for 3 to 4 hours, until the pork is tender and easily pulled apart with a fork.

8. Remove from the oven and let rest for 10 minutes.

9. Pull the pork apart in the baking dish using two forks, then place a generous amount of pulled pork on each brioche bun. Top with tangy coleslaw and extra BBQ sauce, if desired. For lunches, pack the coleslaw on the side!

SLOW COOKER: After searing the pork in step 2, add the pork, onion, garlic, BBQ sauce, and 1 cup (240 ml) chicken broth to a slow cooker and cook on high for 3 to 4 hours, until tender. Procede with step 9.

INGREDIENTS

One 2-pound (906 g) boneless pork shoulder

Kosher salt and black pepper

Vegetable oil

1 yellow onion, finely chopped

3 to 5 garlic cloves, minced

½ cup (120 ml) chicken broth

2 cups (480 ml) BBQ sauce, plus more for serving

2 cups (200 g) Tangy Coleslaw (page 95)

4 to 6 brioche buns

TOOLS

Baking dish

TANGY COLESLAW

15 minutes
Prep time

0 minutes
Cook Time

1 hour and 15 minutes
with chill time
Total Time

Level: ★☆☆☆

Serves 4 to 6

INGREDIENTS

1 small head of cabbage, cored and shredded

2 medium carrots, grated

½ cup (120 ml) mayonnaise

2 tablespoons white vinegar

1 tablespoon Dijon mustard

2 tablespoons sugar, or to taste

½ teaspoon kosher salt

¼ teaspoon black pepper

1. In a large bowl, combine the cabbage and carrots.
2. In a small bowl, whisk the mayonnaise, vinegar, mustard, sugar, salt, and pepper until well combined.
3. Pour the dressing over the cabbage and carrots, and toss until evenly coated. Taste and adjust the sugar, salt, or pepper if needed.
4. Cover the bowl with plastic wrap and refrigerate for at least 1 hour to allow the flavors to meld.
5. Just before serving, give the coleslaw a quick stir to evenly distribute the dressing.

POTATO SALAD

15 minutes
Prep time

25 minutes
Cook Time

1 hour and 40 minutes
with chill time
Total Time

Level: ★☆☆☆

Serves 4 to 6

INGREDIENTS

5 medium Yukon Gold or russet potatoes, chopped

Kosher salt and black pepper

2 to 3 hard-boiled eggs

¼ cup (40 g) chopped onions

¼ cup (25 g) chopped celery

¼ cup (40 g) chopped dill pickles

¼ cup (60 ml) mayonnaise

1 tablespoon Dijon mustard

1. Place the potatoes in a large pot of salted water and bring to a boil. Cook the potatoes until they are tender but not mushy, 10 to 15 minutes. Drain and set aside.
2. While the potatoes are cooking, chop the eggs into small pieces.
3. In a large bowl, combine the onions, celery, pickles, mayonnaise, and mustard.
4. Add the potatoes and the eggs and gently fold everything together until all ingredients are evenly mixed.
5. Taste the potato salad and season with salt and pepper to your liking.
6. You can eat this warm right away or chill the potato salad in the refrigerator for at least 1 hour before serving.

SHRIMP SALAD ROLL + FRESH & FRUITY SALAD

Looking for a light and refreshing lunch or snack? Try this delicious shrimp salad roll! Beat the heat by pairing it with a colorful, customizable, and refreshing fruit salad. To complete this lunch, add some crispy kettle chips.

SHRIMP SALAD ROLL

15 minutes
Prep time

7 minutes
Cook Time

22 minutes
Total Time

Level: ★☆☆☆

Makes 4

INGREDIENTS

1 pound (454 g) peeled and deveined cooked medium (41/50 or 51/60) shrimp

1 celery stalk, finely diced

½ medium tomato, finely diced

½ cup (120 ml) mayonnaise

3 tablespoons chopped fresh parsley

10 garlic cloves, minced, divided

1 tablespoon lemon juice

Kosher salt and black pepper

¼ cup (23 g) grated Parmesan

4 tablespoons butter, softened

4 hoagie rolls

4 butter lettuce leaves

TOOLS

Baking sheet

Parchment paper or aluminum foil

1. Preheat the oven to 375°F (190°C). Line a baking sheet with parchment paper or foil.

2. In a large bowl, mix the shrimp, celery, tomato, mayonnaise, parsley, 2 tablespoons of the minced garlic, lemon juice, salt, and pepper until well combined.

3. In a small bowl, mix the Parmesan, butter, and remaining minced garlic.

4. Slice the rolls lengthwise across the top to create a pocket, being careful not to cut all the way through. Spread the garlic butter mixture evenly onto the rolls. Place them onto the baking sheet.

5. Bake for 5 to 7 minutes, until the bread is golden brown and crispy. Let cool.

6. Lay a leaf of lettuce down on each roll, then divide the shrimp mixture equally among the rolls.

FRESH & FRUITY SALAD

15 minutes
Prep time

15 minutes
Cook Time

30 minutes
Total Time

Level: ★☆☆☆

Serves 3 to 4

INGREDIENTS

3 cups (300 g) chopped fruit (strawberries, blueberries, grapes, pineapple, kiwi, apples, oranges)

2 tablespoons honey

¼ cup (60 ml) fresh orange juice

1 teaspoon fresh lemon juice

1 tablespoon sliced mint leaves

1. Place the fruit in a large bowl.

2. In a small bowl, whisk together the honey, orange juice, and lemon juice.

3. Pour the dressing over the fruit and toss gently to coat evenly.

4. Cover the fruit salad and refrigerate for at least 15 minutes before serving.

5. Garnish with mint leaves and serve.

"All the Small Things" — **Blink 182**

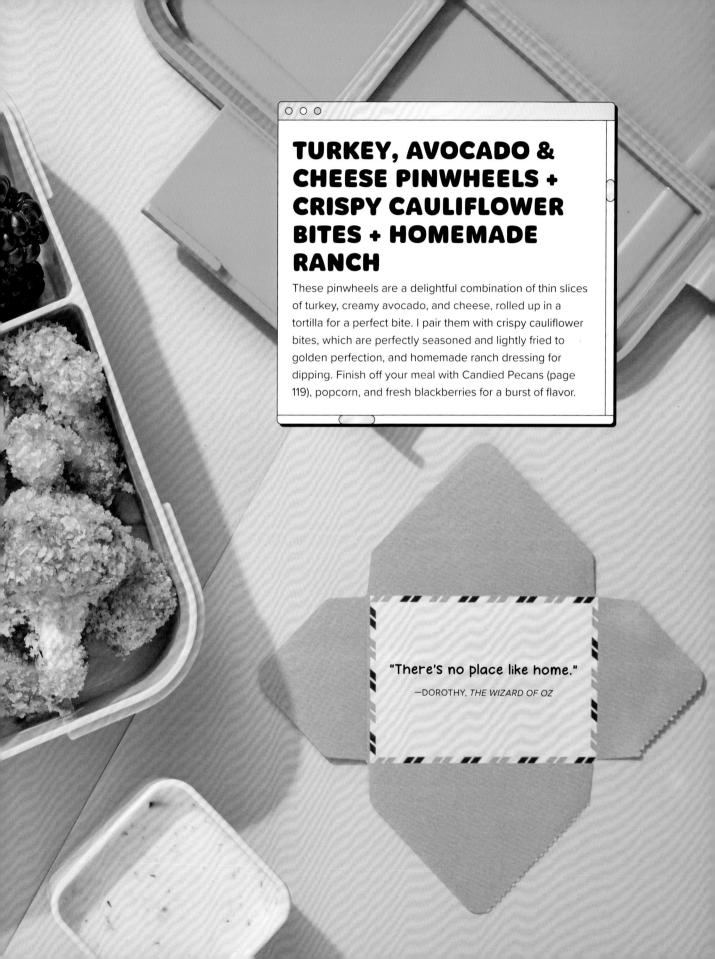

TURKEY, AVOCADO & CHEESE PINWHEELS + CRISPY CAULIFLOWER BITES + HOMEMADE RANCH

These pinwheels are a delightful combination of thin slices of turkey, creamy avocado, and cheese, rolled up in a tortilla for a perfect bite. I pair them with crispy cauliflower bites, which are perfectly seasoned and lightly fried to golden perfection, and homemade ranch dressing for dipping. Finish off your meal with Candied Pecans (page 119), popcorn, and fresh blackberries for a burst of flavor.

"There's no place like home."

—DOROTHY, *THE WIZARD OF OZ*

TURKEY, AVOCADO & CHEESE PINWHEELS

10 minutes
Prep time

0 minutes
Cook Time

25 minutes
with chill time
Total Time

Level: ★☆☆☆	Serves 1 to 2

x

INGREDIENTS

1½ teaspoons
Homemade Ranch
(page 101)

1 large flour tortilla

½ ripe avocado

4 to 5 slices roasted
turkey

2 slices cheddar

Kosher salt and
black pepper

TOOLS

Plastic wrap or
parchment paper

1. Using a spoon, spread the ranch onto the tortilla.

2. Scoop out the avocado flesh, and mash it so it becomes spreadable. Spread it evenly onto the tortilla.

3. Add the turkey and cheese on top, then season with salt and pepper to taste.

4. Roll up the tortilla tightly into a log shape. Wrap it up with plastic wrap or parchment paper.

5. Place in the refrigerator for at least 15 minutes, until firm. Remove the plastic wrap and slice the roll into ½-inch (1cm) rounds.

TIP: When packing these in a lunch, add an ice pack to keep things cool!

CRISPY CAULIFLOWER BITES

10 minutes
Prep time

15 minutes
Cook Time

25 minutes
Total Time

Level: ★☆☆☆

Serves 4

INGREDIENTS

½ cup (60 g) all-purpose flour

½ teaspoon garlic powder

½ teaspoon onion powder

½ teaspoon paprika

¼ teaspoon kosher salt

¼ teaspoon black pepper

1 cup (100 g) panko bread crumbs

½ head of cauliflower, cut into bite-size pieces

Extra virgin olive oil, for drizzling

TOOLS

Air fryer

1. Preheat your air fryer to 375°F (190°C).

2. In a medium bowl, whisk together the flour, garlic powder, onion powder, paprika, salt, and black pepper.

3. Add ½ cup (120 ml) water and whisk until smooth.

4. Place the panko in a separate bowl.

5. Dip each cauliflower piece into the flour mixture, then coat with panko.

6. Place the coated cauliflower pieces on a plate, then drizzle with olive oil.

7. Place the cauliflower bites in the air fryer basket, making sure they are not touching each other. You might need to work in multiple batches, depending on the size of your air fryer.

8. Cook until golden brown and crispy, 12 to 15 minutes, shaking the basket every 5 minutes.

9. Serve warm. When packing for lunch, let cool completely to keep them crispy!

HOMEMADE RANCH

10 minutes
Prep time

0 minutes
Cook Time

1 hour and 10 minutes
with chill time
Total Time

Level: ★☆☆☆

Makes 2 cups (480 ml)

INGREDIENTS

1 cup (240 ml) mayonnaise

½ cup (120 ml) buttermilk

½ cup (120 ml) sour cream

2 tablespoons finely chopped fresh parsley

1 tablespoon finely chopped fresh chives

1 teaspoon dried dill

1 teaspoon garlic powder

1 teaspoon onion powder

½ teaspoon kosher salt

¼ teaspoon black pepper

1. In a medium bowl, whisk the mayonnaise, buttermilk, and sour cream until smooth.

2. Add the parsley, chives, dill, garlic powder, onion powder, salt, and pepper. Stir well.

3. Adjust the consistency by adding more buttermilk, if desired. Taste and adjust the seasoning to your preference.

4. Transfer the dressing to a jar or airtight container. Cover and refrigerate for at least 1 hour before serving to allow the flavors to meld.

5. Stir the dressing before serving, as it may separate slightly in the refrigerator.

6. Store in the refrigerator for up to 1 week. If the dressing thickens after refrigeration, thin it out by adding a little more buttermilk or milk and stir.

CUCUMBER TOAST + EASY SHRIMP-STUFFED AVOCADO

This flavorful combination is perfect for a beautiful meal—it's almost too pretty to eat! The cucumber toast features thinly sliced cucumbers placed on top of slices of toasted bread. Complementing the toast is a shrimp-stuffed avocado, and this lunch is best served with a side of star-shaped puffed cheddar crackers.

CUCUMBER TOAST

10 minutes
Prep time

0 minutes
Cook Time

10 minutes
Total Time

Level: ★☆☆☆   Makes 2

INGREDIENTS

2 slices sandwich bread (white or wheat)

3 tablespoons softened or whipped cream cheese

2 teaspoons lemon juice

1 teaspoon fresh dill leaves, chopped

Kosher salt and black pepper

½ English cucumber, thinly sliced (I like using a peeler)

TOOLS

Vegetable peeler

1. Lightly toast the bread.

2. In a small bowl, mix the cream cheese, lemon juice, dill, salt, and pepper.

3. Spread the cream cheese mixture onto both slices of toast.

4. Place a layer of cucumbers over the toast, slightly overlapping each other.

5. Top with additional fresh dill and a sprinkle of black pepper. Cut into halves or quarters and serve.

SPECIAL TOUCHES: Add tiny little carrot and bell pepper flowers to adorn your cucumber toast.

EASY SHRIMP—STUFFED AVOCADO

15 minutes
Prep time

0 minutes
Cook Time

15 minutes
Total Time

Level: ★☆☆☆   Serves 4

INGREDIENTS

½ pound (227 g) raw shrimp, peeled and deveined

2 ripe avocados, halved lengthwise and pitted

¼ cup (40 g) finely chopped red onion

¼ cup (30 g) finely chopped red bell pepper

1 tablespoon chopped fresh cilantro

3 tablespoons mayonnaise

1 tablespoon lime juice

Kosher salt and black pepper

1. Bring a large pot of water to a boil. Add the shrimp and cook until pink and cooked through, 2 to 3 minutes. Let cool for a few minutes, then cut into bite-size pieces.

3. Scoop out a little bit of the flesh from each avocado half to make room for the filling (use the flesh for another purpose).

4. In a medium bowl, combine the shrimp, onion, bell pepper, and cilantro. Add the mayonnaise, lime juice, salt, and black pepper and mix well.

5. Spoon the shrimp mixture into the avocado halves.

6. Serve immediately and enjoy!

"Last Nite" — **The Strokes**

BUFFALO CHICKEN SANDWICHES + PICKLE CHIPS

Crispy, tender chicken coated in zesty buffalo sauce is served on a soft bun with lettuce and tomato with a side of creamy ranch dressing. It's the perfect balance of spicy and savory. Serve with crispy pickle chips, fried to perfection, and bite-size melon balls. This combo is absolutely mouthwatering!

You are one in a melon.
Have the best day today!

BUFFALO CHICKEN SANDWICHES

10 minutes
Prep time

20 minutes
Cook Time

30 minutes
Total Time

Level: ★★☆☆

Makes 4

1. Preheat the oven to 375°F (190°C).

2. Season both sides of the chicken with salt and pepper, then dredge the chicken in the flour until completely coated.

3. Melt the butter in a large skillet over medium-high heat.

4. Add the chicken to the skillet and cook until golden brown, 4 to 5 minutes per side. Transfer the chicken to a baking sheet.

5. Brush the chicken with the Buffalo sauce.

6. Bake until the chicken is cooked through, 10 to 12 minutes.

7. Toast the hamburger buns, then place the chicken on the bottom half of each bun.

8. Top the chicken with blue cheese or ranch dressing, lettuce, and tomato, if desired.

9. Cover with the top half of the bun and serve immediately or cool completely before adding to your lunch!

SPECIAL TOUCHES: Don't forget to add food picks. Not only do they make your sandwich look cuter, but they also hold the sandwich in place.

INGREDIENTS

2 chicken breasts

Kosher salt and black pepper

½ cup (60 g) all-purpose flour

2 tablespoons butter

½ cup (120 ml) Buffalo sauce

4 Brioche hamburger buns

Blue cheese or ranch dressing, optional

Lettuce and tomato, optional

TOOLS

Baking sheet

PICKLE CHIPS

10 minutes
Prep time

10 minutes
Cook Time

20 minutes
Total Time

Level: ★★☆☆

Serves 4

1. In a shallow dish, whisk together the flour, paprika, garlic powder, onion powder, salt, and black pepper.

2. Dip each pickle slice into the buttermilk, then coat in the seasoned flour mixture.

3. Heat about 1 inch (2.5 cm) of vegetable oil in a large skillet over medium heat.

4. Fry the pickles in batches until golden brown, turning occasionally, 2 to 3 minutes.

5. Transfer the fried pickles to paper towels to drain any excess oil.

6. Serve hot with fry sauce or cool completely before adding to a lunch!

INGREDIENTS

2 cups (240 g) all-purpose flour

1 teaspoon paprika

1 teaspoon garlic powder

1 teaspoon onion powder

1 teaspoon salt

½ teaspoon black pepper

1½ cups (300 g) dill pickle slices, patted dry

1 cup (240 ml) buttermilk

Vegetable oil, for frying

Easy Fry Sauce (page 89), for serving

SLIDERS WITH CARAMELIZED ONIONS + HOT CHEETO MOZZARELLA STICKS

These easy-to-make sliders offer sweetness from the onions, which complement the juicy meat perfectly. Pair them with Hot Cheeto mozzarella sticks, a twist on the classic snack, where gooey mozzarella cheese is coated in a crunchy Hot Cheeto crust. Enjoy a side of pickles to add a tangy and refreshing touch.

SLIDERS WITH CARAMELIZED ONIONS

10 minutes
Prep time

40 minutes
Cook Time

50 minutes
Total Time

Level: ★★☆☆

Makes 8

INGREDIENTS

3 tablespoons butter, divided

1 tablespoon olive oil

2 large yellow onions, sliced

1 teaspoon brown sugar

¼ cup (60 ml) beef broth

1 pound (454 g) ground beef

Kosher salt and black pepper

8 slices cheddar or American cheese

8 slider buns

Mayonnaise

TOOLS

Grill or grill pan

1. Heat 2 tablespoons of butter and the olive oil in a large skillet over medium heat until the butter melts. Add the onions and stir to coat. Add a pinch of salt.

2. Cook slowly, stirring occasionally, until soft and caramelized, 20 to 25 minutes. After 10 minutes, stir in the brown sugar.

3. Stir in the beef broth. Cook until the liquid has evaporated and the onions are sticky and sweet, 5 to 10 minutes.

4. Meanwhile, preheat your grill to medium-high heat.

5. Divide the ground beef into eight equal portions and shape them into mini patties. Season both sides of each patty with salt and pepper.

6. Add 1 tablespoon butter to the grill. Grill the patties until they're cooked to your preference, 2 to 3 minutes per side. During the last minute of cooking time, add a slice of cheese to each patty, and cover with a lid to melt.

7. To assemble the sliders, spread mayo on the bottom bun, add a patty, and top with caramelized onions.

HOT CHEETO MOZZARELLA STICKS

20 minutes
Prep time

10 minutes
Cook Time

30 minutes
Total Time

Level: ★★☆☆

Makes 12

INGREDIENTS

6 mozzarella cheese sticks, halved crosswise

One 3.25-ounce (92 g) bag Hot Cheetos

½ cup (60 g) all-purpose flour

1 egg, beaten

1 tablespoons milk

Kosher salt and black pepper

Vegetable oil

1. Preheat 1 inch (2.5 cm) of oil in a medium pot to 375°F (190°C).

2. Crush the Hot Cheetos in a plastic bag until they are finely crushed.

3. Set up three bowls for the breading station: one with the flour, one with the beaten eggs and milk, and one with the crushed Cheetos.

4. Season the flour with salt and pepper to taste.

5. Take a cheese stick and coat it in the flour mixture, then the egg mixture, and finally the Cheetos.

6. Repeat with the remaining cheese sticks.

7. Fry in the hot oil, in batches, until golden brown, 2 to 3 minutes.

8. Drain on a paper towel–lined plate.

AIR FRYER: Spray the air fryer basket with nonstick cooking spray. Place the coated cheese sticks in a single layer in the air fryer basket, without overcrowding.

Cook at 400°F (200°C) for 6 to 8 minutes, until golden brown. Flip halfway through for even browning.

Remove the mozzarella sticks and let cool for a few minutes before serving.

"Nine in the Afternoon" — **Panic! at the Disco**

"The most beautiful thing you can wear is confidence."

—BLAKE LIVELY

CHICKEN TAQUITOS + SUMMER SALSA + CHURRO TORTILLA CHIPS

This ultimate lunch pairs chicken taquitos with a vibrant summer salsa and sweet churro tortilla chips. The savory taquitos are crispy perfection; they're generously filled with chicken, ensuring every bite is a burst of flavor. Serve with sour cream and guacamole on the side, and enhance the flavors by squeezing some limes over your meal. For the perfect finish, pack some crunchy toasted corn nuts.

CHICKEN TAQUITOS

15 minutes
Prep time

15 minutes
Cook Time

30 minutes
Total Time

Level: ★★☆☆

Makes 8 to 10

1. Heat the olive oil in a large skillet over medium-high heat. Add the chicken and season with cumin, chili powder, garlic powder, onion powder, salt, and pepper. Cook until no longer pink, stirring occasionally, 8 to 10 minutes.

2. Remove the chicken from the skillet and shred into small pieces. You can use two forks, but I like using a hand mixer to shred it more quickly.

3. In a large bowl, mix the chicken, cream cheese, and cheddar.

4. Place a few tablespoons of the chicken mixture in the center of a tortilla. Roll up the tortilla tightly and secure with toothpicks. Repeat with the remaining tortillas and chicken mixture.

5. Heat enough vegetable oil to coat the taquitos in a large frying pan. Add the taquitos carefully and fry until golden brown, 2 to 3 minutes per side. Remove from the oil and drain on a paper towel.

6. Serve with guacamole, sour cream, and salsa for dipping. Garnish with cilantro and lime wedges.

INGREDIENTS

1 tablespoon olive oil

1 pound (454 g) chicken breast

½ teaspoon ground cumin

½ teaspoon chili powder

¼ teaspoon garlic powder

¼ teaspoon onion powder

Kosher salt and black pepper

3 ounces (85 g) cream cheese, softened

½ cup (55 g) shredded cheddar

8 to 10 medium flour tortillas

Vegetable oil

FOR SERVING

Guacamole

Sour cream

Summer Salsa (page 113)

Cilantro leaves

Lime wedges

TOOLS

Hand mixer

Toothpicks

SUMMER SALSA

20 minutes
Prep time

30 minutes
Cook Time

50 minutes
Total Time

Level: ★☆☆☆   **Makes 4 cups (1 kg)**

INGREDIENTS

4 ripe medium tomatoes, diced

1 mango, peeled and diced or one 15-ounce (425 g) can diced mangoes

1 small red onion, diced

1½ cups (330 g) canned pineapple, diced

1 jalapeño, seeded and minced

½ cup (8 g) chopped fresh cilantro leaves

3 tablespoons canned pineapple juice

¼ cup (60 ml) fresh lime juice

½ teaspoon kosher salt

1. In a large bowl, combine the tomatoes, mango, onion, pineapple, jalapeño, and cilantro.
2. Add the pineapple juice, lime juice, and salt to the bowl and stir until well combined.
3. Cover the bowl and chill in the refrigerator for at least 30 minutes before serving.
4. Serve as a dip or topping for your favorite dishes.

CHURRO TORTILLA CHIPS ⋮

5 minutes
Prep time

20 minutes
Cook Time

25 minutes
Total Time

Level: ★☆☆☆   **Serves 2 to 4**

INGREDIENTS

8 small soft flour tortillas

3 tablespoons sugar

1 teaspoon ground cinnamon

2 tablespoons unsalted butter, melted

TOOLS

Baking sheet

1. Preheat the oven to 350°F (175°C).
2. Cut the tortillas into quarters and lay them out on a baking sheet.
3. In a small bowl, combine the sugar and cinnamon.
4. Brush the tortillas with melted butter on one side, and then sprinkle generously with the cinnamon-sugar mixture.
5. Bake for 15 to 20 minutes, until crispy and golden brown.

CUCUMBER VEGGIE ROLLS + PEANUT DIPPING SAUCE

Cucumber veggie rolls, served with flavorful peanut dipping sauce, make for a refreshing and wonderful meal. These light and crisp rolls are filled with fresh vegetables, offering a burst of flavors and textures. For the side, watermelon blueberry flowers create an eye-catching addition to your lunch.

CUCUMBER VEGGIE ROLLS

15 minutes
Prep time

0 minutes
Cook Time

15 minutes
Total Time

Level: ★★☆☆	Serves 2

INGREDIENTS

2 large cucumbers

½ firm avocado

¼ red bell pepper, julienned

¼ yellow bell pepper, julienned

¼ carrot, julienned

TOOLS

Apple corer

1. Halve the cucumbers widthwise. Using an apple corer, remove the center of the cucumbers.

2. Stuff a few pieces of avocado, red bell pepper, yellow bell pepper, and carrot into the cucumbers until they are fully packed.

3. Slice the cucumbers into ½-inch-thick (1 cm) pieces.

4. Serve chilled.

PEANUT DIPPING SAUCE

10 minutes
Prep time

3 minutes
Cook Time

13 minutes
Total Time

Level: ★☆☆☆	Makes 1 cup (240 ml)

INGREDIENTS

½ cup (125 g) creamy peanut butter

¼ cup (60 ml) soy sauce

¼ cup (60 ml) rice vinegar

2 tablespoons honey

2 garlic cloves, minced

1 teaspoon sesame oil

¼ teaspoon red pepper flakes, optional

¼ cup (60 ml) warm water

Chopped peanuts and sesame seeds

1. In a medium bowl, whisk together the peanut butter, soy sauce, vinegar, honey, garlic, sesame oil, and red pepper flakes, if using.

2. Transfer the sauce to a small pot and simmer over medium-low heat for 1 minute.

3. While whisking continuously, slowly pour in the warm water. Simmer until the sauce reaches your desired consistency, another 1 to 2 minutes. You may need to adjust the amount of water according to your preference.

4. Taste and adjust the seasoning as needed. Add more soy sauce or honey to achieve the perfect balance of salty and sweet.

5. Transfer to a serving bowl and garnish with chopped peanuts and sesame seeds. Perfect for dipping veggies!

"Heat Waves" — **Glass Animals**

You are capable of amazing things.

MOZZARELLA, TOMATO & SPINACH PESTO PANINI + BERRY SUMMER SALAD + CANDIED PECANS

This delectable sandwich features melted mozzarella, fresh tomatoes, and a flavorful spinach pesto spread. The refreshing summer salad is bursting with juicy berries, crisp greens, and a tangy vinaigrette dressing. Serve candied pecans on the side, to add on top of your salad so it stays fresh and crunchy.

MOZZARELLA, TOMATO & SPINACH PESTO PANINI

5 minutes
Prep time

7 minutes
Cook Time

12 minutes
Total Time

Level: ★★☆☆	Makes 1

1. Preheat your panini press, grill, or griddle to medium-high heat.

2. Spread the pesto on the insides of the top and bottom of the bread.

3. Layer the spinach, tomato, and mozzarella on the bottom of the bread, on top of the pesto. Sprinkle with salt and pepper to taste, then top with the other half of the bread.

4. Lightly butter the top of the bread.

5. Place the sandwich on the panini press and cook until the bread is golden brown and the cheese has melted, 3 to 5 minutes.

6. Remove from the heat and let the sandwich cool for a minute, then cut into halves or quarters and serve hot or cool to pack for lunch.

INGREDIENTS

1 small ciabatta loaf, halved lengthwise

¼ cup (60 ml) basil pesto

1 cup (30 g) baby spinach leaves

1 large tomato, sliced

8 ounces (227 g) fresh mozzarella, sliced

Kosher salt and black pepper

Butter

TOOLS

Panini press, grill, or griddle

BERRY SUMMER SALAD

10 minutes Prep time **0 minutes** Cook Time **10 minutes** Total Time

Level: ★☆☆☆ Serves 2

INGREDIENTS

4 cups (140 g) mixed greens

½ cup (40 g) sliced strawberries

¼ cup (40 g) blueberries

¼ cup (30 g) raspberries

¼ cup (60 g) crumbled goat cheese

3 tablespoons olive oil

2 tablespoons balsamic vinegar

Kosher salt and black pepper

1. Place the mixed greens in a large salad bowl.
2. Add the strawberries, blueberries, raspberries, and goat cheese.
3. If serving right away, drizzle the olive oil and balsamic vinegar over the top of the salad and toss to mix.
4. If packing in a lunch, mix the oil and vinegar in a small container and serve on the side.
5. Season with salt and pepper. Enjoy!

CANDIED PECANS

5 minutes Prep time **15 minutes** Cook Time **20 minutes** Total Time

Level: ★☆☆☆ Makes 2 cups (240 g)

INGREDIENTS

¼ cup (60 ml) maple syrup

¼ cup (55 g) brown sugar

½ teaspoon ground cinnamon

¼ teaspoon kosher salt

2 cups (240 g) pecan halves

TOOLS

Baking sheet

Parchment paper

1. Preheat the oven to 350°F (175°C). Line a baking sheet with parchment paper.
2. In a medium bowl, mix the maple syrup, brown sugar, cinnamon, and salt.
3. Add the pecan halves to the bowl and stir to coat evenly. Spread the pecans in a single layer on the baking sheet.
4. Bake for 10 to 15 minutes, stirring occasionally, until golden brown and fragrant.
5. Remove from the oven and allow the pecans to cool completely before using or storing in an airtight container at room temperature for up to 2 weeks.

GRILLED CHEESE SAMMY + ROASTED TOMATO SOUP

This grilled cheese sammy and roasted tomato soup combo is one of Addy's favorite lunches. It's like a big hug in a meal. To balance some of the richness, I serve this with a side of star-cut grapes. This lunch is the perfect hearty and comforting meal.

GRILLED CHEESE SAMMY

5 minutes
Prep time

6 minutes
Cook Time

11 minutes
Total Time

Level: ★☆☆☆

Makes 1

INGREDIENTS

2 slices Texas toast or thick sandwich bread

1 tablespoon butter

2 slices medium cheddar

1 slice smoked Gouda

x

1. Preheat a nonstick skillet over medium heat.
2. Spread the butter on one side of each slice of bread.
3. Place the cheddar and Gouda onto the unbuttered side of one slice of bread, making sure the cheese does not extend over the edges.
4. Top with the other slice of bread, buttered side up.
5. Place the sandwich in the skillet and cook until the bottom is golden brown and crisp, 2 to 3 minutes.
6. Gently flip the sandwich and continue cooking until the other side is golden brown and the cheese is melted, 2 to 3 minutes.
7. Remove from the skillet, slice into halves or quarters, and serve.

AIR FRYER: Cook in the air fryer at 330°F (165°C) for 3 minutes. Flip over and cook for another 3 minutes, until golden brown.

ROASTED TOMATO SOUP

15 minutes
Prep time

45 minutes
Cook Time

1 hour
Total Time

Level: ★☆☆☆

Serves 4

INGREDIENTS

6 large tomatoes, halved

½ yellow onion, peeled

1 head of garlic, halved crosswise

2 fresh thyme sprigs

Olive oil

Kosher salt and black pepper

4 cups (960 ml) vegetable or chicken broth

1 tablespoon tomato paste

1 teaspoon dried oregano

½ cup (120 ml) heavy cream, plus more for serving

Fresh basil or parsley

TOOLS

Baking sheet

Blender or food processor

x

1. Preheat the oven to 425°F (220°C).
2. Place the tomatoes, onion, garlic, and thyme onto a baking sheet. Drizzle with olive oil and season with salt and pepper.
3. Roast for 45 minutes, until soft and slightly charred.
4. Remove the tomato and garlic skins, then transfer the roasted vegetables to a blender or food processor. Add the vegetable broth and blend until smooth.
5. Pour the mixture into a large pot, then add the tomato paste and oregano and bring to a boil. Reduce the heat and simmer for 10 to 15 minutes.
8. Stir in the heavy cream, and cook for an additional 5 minutes, stirring occasionally. Taste the soup and adjust the seasoning if necessary.
9. Garnish with fresh basil or parsley and a drizzle of heavy cream. Serve hot.

You are my definition of perfect!

"Say You'll Be There" — **Spice Girls**

CRISPY SALMON RICE PAPER BITES + SOY DIPPING SAUCE + BLISTERED TERIYAKI SHISHITO PEPPERS

These bite-size crispy salmon rice paper bites are paired perfectly with a flavorful soy dipping sauce. A side of blistered teriyaki shishito peppers adds a tiny touch of heat and sweetness. So good!

CRISPY SALMON RICE PAPER BITES

10 minutes
Prep time

12 minutes
Cook Time

22 minutes
Total Time

Level: ★★☆☆	Makes 6 to 10

INGREDIENTS

12 ounces (340 g) boneless, skinless salmon

1 tablespoon avocado oil

Kosher salt and black pepper

6 to 10 pieces rice paper

1 bunch green onions, cut into 1- to 2-inch (2.5 to 5 cm) pieces

Soy Dipping Sauce (page 125), for serving

1. Pat dry your salmon and cut into bite-size (about 1-inch/2.5 cm) pieces.

2. In a medium nonstick pan over medium heat, preheat the oil.

3. Season both sides of your salmon with salt and pepper and then add to the pan, searing on each side for 3 to 4 minutes.

4. Lightly dunk a piece of rice paper in a bowl of cold water until pliable and start assembling your wraps. Add a piece of salmon in the middle and top it with two to three pieces of green onion.

5. Then start carefully wrapping! Fold in the bottom and then the sides, and then roll the salmon upward. Repeat the process with remaining pieces of salmon.

6. To the same pan with oil from the salmon, add the salmon bites. Cook over medium heat until golden brown and crispy, about 1 minute on each side.

7. Remove from the heat and serve with soy dipping sauce!

SOY DIPPING SAUCE

5 minutes
Prep time

0 minutes
Cook Time

5 minutes
Total Time

Level: ★☆☆☆

Makes ½ cup (120 ml)

INGREDIENTS

- ¼ cup (60 ml) soy sauce
- 2 tablespoons sesame oil
- 1 tablespoon white vinegar
- 1 tablespoon sugar or honey
- 1½ teaspoons gochugaru (Korean red pepper flakes), optional for a little spice
- 1 teaspoon sesame seeds
- 1 pinch chopped fresh cilantro

1. In a small bowl, combine the soy sauce, sesame oil, vinegar, sugar, gochugaru (if using), sesame seeds, and cilantro. Mix well.

BLISTERED TERIYAKI SHISHITO PEPPERS

5 minutes
Prep time

7 minutes
Cook Time

13 minutes
Total Time

Level: ★☆☆☆

Serves 4

INGREDIENTS

- 2 tablespoons vegetable oil
- 1 pound (454 g) shishito peppers
- 1 tablespoon soy sauce
- 1 tablespoon oyster sauce
- 1 tablespoon sugar or honey
- Sesame seeds (optional)

1. Heat the oil in a large skillet over medium-high heat.
2. Add the peppers and cook until they start to blister and char on the outside, 3 to 4 minutes, stirring occasionally.
3. Meanwhile, combine the soy sauce, oyster sauce, and sugar in a small bowl. Mix well.
4. Reduce the heat to medium-low and drizzle the sauce over the peppers. Toss gently to coat.
5. Continue cooking until the peppers are tender and the sauce has slightly caramelized, 1 to 2 minutes. Transfer the peppers to a serving dish.
6. Sprinkle sesame seeds over the peppers and serve!

DINNER LEFTOVERS

“Lucky” — **Britney Spears**

The only person you should try to be better than is the person you were yesterday.

HEARTY HOMESTYLE CHILI

15 minutes
Prep time

45 minutes
Cook Time

1 hour
Total Time

Level: ★★☆☆

Serves 6

1. Heat the oil in a large pot over medium heat. Add the onion and garlic and sauté until the onions are translucent, 3 to 5 minutes.

2. Add the beef and cook until browned, breaking it up into small pieces, 5 to 7 minutes. Season with salt and pepper to taste.

3. Add the bell peppers and sauté for 1 minute.

4. Add the stewed and crushed tomatoes and stir well to combine. Stir in the beans, jalapeño, and habanero.

5. Add the chili powder, cumin, garlic powder, onion powder, sugar, and oregano. Stir well, then add salt and pepper to taste.

6. Reduce the heat to low, cover, and simmer for 30 to 45 minutes, stirring occasionally, until thickened.

7. Ladle the chili into bowls and top with your preferred toppings.

INGREDIENTS

2 tablespoons vegetable oil

1 small yellow onion, diced

4 garlic cloves, minced

1 to 1½ pounds (454 to 680 g) ground beef

Kosher salt and black pepper

1 red bell pepper, diced

1 green bell pepper, diced

1 yellow bell pepper, diced

Two 15-ounce (425 g) cans stewed tomatoes

One 15-ounce (425 g) can crushed tomatoes

One 15-ounce (425 g) can red kidney beans, drained and rinsed

1 jalapeño, finely diced

1 habanero, finely diced

¼ cup (24 g) chili powder

2½ teaspoons ground cumin

2 teaspoons garlic powder

2 teaspoons onion powder

1½ teaspoons sugar

1 teaspoon dried oregano

FOR SERVING (OPTIONAL)

Shredded cheese

Sour cream

Chopped green onion

Chopped yellow onion

Butter crackers

Classic Cornbread (page 131)

CLASSIC CORNBREAD

10 minutes
Prep time

25 minutes
Cook Time

35 minutes
Total Time

Level: ★★☆☆

Serves 4

INGREDIENTS

Butter, for greasing

1 cup (120 g) cornmeal

1 cup (120 g) all-purpose flour

¼ cup (50 g) sugar

1 tablespoon baking powder

½ teaspoon kosher salt

1 cup (240 g) canned cream-style corn

½ cup (120 ml) milk

¼ cup (60 ml) melted butter

2 large eggs

TOOLS

Baking dish

1. Preheat the oven to 400°F (200°C) and grease an 8-inch (20 cm) square baking dish with butter.

2. In a large bowl, whisk together the cornmeal, flour, sugar, baking powder, and salt.

3. In a medium bowl, combine the corn, milk, melted butter, and eggs.

4. Pour the wet ingredients into the dry ingredients and stir until just combined. Do not overmix; a few lumps are fine.

5. Transfer the batter into the baking dish, spreading it out evenly.

6. Bake until the top is golden brown and a toothpick inserted into the center comes out clean, 20 to 25 minutes.

7. Remove from the oven and let cool for a few minutes before slicing and serving.

WHIPPED HONEY BUTTER

5 minutes
Prep time

0 minutes
Cook Time

5 minutes
Total Time

Level: ★☆☆☆

Makes: ½ cup (75 g)

INGREDIENTS

8 tablespoons unsalted butter, softened

2 tablespoons honey

Pinch of flaky salt, optional

1. In a medium bowl, use a hand mixer (or stand mixer) to beat the butter on medium speed until creamy and smooth.

2. Add the honey and beat on medium speed until the honey is fully incorporated and the butter is light and fluffy. If desired, add a pinch of salt to enhance the flavors.

3. Transfer the honey butter to a serving dish or shape into a log using plastic wrap or parchment paper.

4. Chill in the fridge or serve right away.

In a world where you can be anything, be kind.

"Alive" – **Empire of the Sun**

COLORFUL PASTA SALAD + HOMEMADE ITALIAN DRESSING + CRUNCHY GARLIC CROUTONS

Indulge in this delightful pasta salad with homemade Italian dressing. Serve the crunchy garlic croutons on the side, so they don't get soggy, and add little cheeses with cute heart and star cutouts, everything-seasoned crackers, and a few orange slices for a meal that will leave you completely satisfied.

COLORFUL PASTA SALAD

15 minutes
Prep time

10 minutes
Cook Time

25 minutes
Total Time

Level: ★☆☆☆

Serves 4 to 6

INGREDIENTS

12 ounces (340 g) tricolor rotini

1 cup (90 g) cut broccoli florets

½ red bell pepper, julienned

½ green bell pepper, julienned

½ cup (120 g) sliced salami, julienned

½ cup (125 g) sliced pepperoni, julienned

½ cup (110 g) artichoke hearts, sliced

½ cup (40 g) sun-dried tomatoes in olive oil, chopped

½ cup (35 g) black olives, sliced

Kosher salt and black pepper

⅓ cup (80 ml) Homemade Italian Dressing (page 135)

Crunchy Garlic Croutons (page 135)

Chopped fresh parsley, optional

1. Cook the pasta according to package directions, until al dente. Drain and rinse under cold water, then set aside.

2. To a large bowl, add the broccoli, bell peppers, salami, pepperoni, artichoke hearts, sun-dried tomatoes, and olives. Add salt and black pepper to taste.

3. Add the pasta and the dressing. Stir well to coat.

4. Enjoy right away or cover the bowl with plastic wrap and refrigerate for at least 30 minutes to allow the flavors to blend.

5. Before serving, top with croutons and give the pasta salad a good stir. Garnish with fresh parsley, if desired.

HOMEMADE ITALIAN DRESSING

10 minutes
Prep time

0 minutes
Cook Time

10 minutes
Total Time

Level: ★☆☆☆

Makes 1 cup (240 ml)

INGREDIENTS

½ cup (120 ml) olive oil

¼ cup (60 ml) red wine vinegar

2 tablespoons fresh lemon juice

1 tablespoon Dijon mustard

1 teaspoon honey

1 garlic clove, minced

½ teaspoon dried oregano

¼ teaspoon dried basil

¼ teaspoon dried thyme

Kosher salt and black pepper

1. In a small bowl, whisk the olive oil, vinegar, lemon juice, mustard, and honey.

2. Add the garlic, oregano, basil, thyme, and salt and pepper to taste. Whisk until well combined.

3. Serve immediately or store in an airtight container in the refrigerator for up to 2 weeks.

CRUNCHY GARLIC CROUTONS

5 minutes
Prep time

15 minutes
Cook Time

20 minutes
Total Time

Level: ★☆☆☆

Makes 2 cups (240 g)

INGREDIENTS

2 cups (240 g) cubed bread (preferably stale)

2 to 3 tablespoons olive oil

2 garlic cloves, minced

Kosher salt and black pepper

TOOLS

Baking sheet

1. Preheat the oven to 375°F (190°C).

2. In a large bowl, combine the bread, olive oil, and garlic. Mix well to coat. Season with salt and pepper to taste.

3. Spread the bread cubes onto a baking sheet in a single layer.

4. Bake for 10 to 15 minutes, until golden brown and crispy.

5. Remove from the oven and let cool completely before serving.

CRAB-STUFFED MUSHROOMS + SMOKED SALMON DIP

Enjoy a delicious seafood lunch featuring crab-stuffed mushrooms and a creamy smoked salmon dip. These are also a hit at parties! Complete your meal with wafer crisps, carrots, and snap peas, which are a tasty accompaniment to the flavorful salmon dip.

CRAB—STUFFED MUSHROOMS

15 minutes
Prep time

20 minutes
Cook Time

35 minutes
Total Time

Level: ★★☆☆

Serves 4

INGREDIENTS

Nonstick cooking spray

½ pound (227 g) fresh lump crabmeat

4 ounces (113 g) cream cheese, softened

¼ cup (25 g) grated Parmesan

2 tablespoons finely chopped green onions

1 teaspoon Worcestershire sauce

¼ teaspoon garlic powder

Kosher salt and black pepper

1 pound (454 g) large cremini or button mushrooms, stemmed

½ lemon

TOOLS

Baking sheet

1. Preheat the oven to 375°F (190°C). Spray a baking sheet with nonstick cooking spray.

2. In a large bowl, combine the crab, cream cheese, Parmesan, green onions, Worcestershire sauce, garlic powder, salt, and pepper. Mix well.

3. Stuff each mushroom cap with 1 to 2 tablespoonfuls of the mixture. You want them to be a little overstuffed, but the mixture shouldn't be falling out.

4. Transfer the mushrooms to the baking sheet and bake for 15 to 20 minutes, until golden brown and heated through.

5. Squeeze lemon juice on top of the mushrooms. Serve warm and enjoy! Cool completely for lunches.

SMOKED SALMON DIP

10 minutes
Prep time

30 minutes
Chill Time

40 minutes
Total Time

Level: ★☆☆☆

Makes 1½ cups (400 g)

INGREDIENTS

8 ounces (227 g) cream cheese, softened

4 ounces (113 g) smoked salmon, chopped

¼ cup (60 ml) sour cream

1 tablespoon lemon juice

1 tablespoon chopped fresh dill

Kosher salt and black pepper

FOR SERVING

Crackers

Chips

Raw vegetable sticks

1. In a medium bowl, beat the cream cheese until smooth.

2. Add in the salmon, sour cream, lemon juice, and dill, and mix well. Season with salt and pepper.

3. Cover the bowl and refrigerate for at least 30 minutes to allow the flavors to meld.

4. Serve with crackers, chips, or raw vegetable sticks.

You are the cheese
to my macaroni.

◀◀ ▶❙❙ ▶▶

"Kiss Me" – **Sixpence None The Richer**

TUNA MAC & CHEESE + SMASHED BRUSSELS SPROUTS

Tuna mac and cheese (my girls' favorite) and smashed brussel sprouts make up this comforting lunch. One of my favorite memories from my time working in retail was sharing homemade lunches with my coworkers for our lunch breaks, and my friend Megan would bring in her tuna mac and cheese. I've been hooked ever since. For the sides, I've added yogurt-covered raisins, mini chocolates and gummy bears, watermelon hearts, walnuts, and banana chips, for a mix of sweetness and crunch.

TUNA MAC & CHEESE

10 minutes
Prep time

25 minutes
Cook Time

35 minutes
Total Time

Level: ★★☆☆		Serves 4

1. Cook the macaroni according to package directions. Drain and set aside.

2. In a medium saucepan over medium heat, melt the butter. Whisk in the flour until it forms a paste. Continue to cook for about 1 minute.

3. Gradually add in the milk, whisking constantly to avoid clumps. Bring the mixture to a simmer until the sauce has thickened, 5 to 7 minutes.

4. Stir in 2 cups (226 g) cheddar until it has melted into the sauce.

5. Add the tuna, macaroni, dill, and cayenne (if you like a little heat) to the saucepan. Stir to combine, then season with salt and pepper to taste.

6. Top with the remaining cheddar cheese.

7. Transfer the mixture into a baking dish and broil on high in the oven for 3 to 5 minutes, until the top is golden brown and the cheese is melted. Make sure to keep an eye on your broiler so the cheese doesn't burn.

8. Remove from the oven and let cool for a few minutes before serving. Top with black pepper and fresh dill, if desired.

INGREDIENTS

1 pound (454 g) macaroni or shells

3 tablespoons butter

3 tablespoons all-purpose flour

2½ cups (600 ml) milk or heavy cream

2⅓ cups (263 g) shredded cheddar, divided

Two 5-ounce (142 g) cans tuna in water, drained

1 teaspoon dried dill

Cayenne, optional

Kosher salt and black pepper

Fresh dill, for garnish, optional

TOOLS

Baking dish

SMASHED BRUSSELS SPROUTS

15 minutes	**30 minutes**	**45 minutes**
Prep time	Cook Time	Total Time

Level: ★☆☆☆ **Serves 4**

1. Preheat your oven to 400°F (200°C). Line a baking sheet with parchment paper.

2. Add the Brussels sprouts and sea salt to a large pot of boiling water. Boil until slightly tender and bright green, 7 to 10 minutes. Drain and pat dry with a paper towel.

3. In a large bowl, toss the sprouts with the olive oil, vinegar, salt, and pepper.

4. Spread the sprouts evenly, cut side down, on the baking sheet, making sure not to overcrowd them.

5. Using the bottom of a mason jar or a potato masher, press down on the sprouts to smash them flat.

6. Roast the sprouts for 20 minutes, until the bottoms are crispy and golden brown.

7. Drizzle the hot honey over the sprouts. Serve immediately while still warm. Cool completely to keep their crispness for lunches.

INGREDIENTS

1 pound (454 g) Brussels sprouts, trimmed and halved

2 teaspoons sea salt

2 tablespoons olive oil

2 tablespoons balsamic vinegar

Kosher salt and black pepper

1 tablespoon hot honey

TOOLS

Baking sheet

Parchment paper

"Electric Feel" — MGMT

Do what makes your soul shine.

CHICKEN TORTILLA SOUP + HOMEMADE TORTILLA CHIPS + GUACAMOLE

This hearty chicken tortilla soup, filled with tender chicken, vegetables, and aromatic spices, is on my monthly rotation. It's a meal that will satisfy the whole family. Add avocado slices, lime wedges, and radishes for the toppings on the side and serve with crunchy tortilla chips, creamy guacamole, and slices of juicy mango.

CHICKEN TORTILLA SOUP

15 minutes
Prep time

4 hours
Cook Time

4 hours and 15 minutes
Total Time

Level: ★★☆☆

Serves 6

1. In a large pot, heat the oil over medium heat. Add the carrots, onion, bell peppers, and garlic. Sauté until softened, 3 to 5 minutes.

2. Add the chicken and pour in the stewed tomatoes, along with their juices.

3. Dissolve the bouillon in 3 cups (720 ml) water and add to the pot.

4. Stir in the cayenne, salt, black pepper, chili powder, cumin, garlic powder, oregano, onion powder, paprika, and red pepper flakes.

5. Bring to a boil, then reduce the heat to low and let simmer for 3½ to 4 hours.

6. Carefully remove the chicken from the pot and shred the meat using two forks. Discard the bones. Return the shredded chicken to the pot and stir it into the soup.

7. Serve, topped with tortilla chips, green onions, a squeeze of lime, a dollop of crema, avocado slices, a sprinkle of cheese, and cilantro.

INGREDIENTS

2 to 3 tablespoons vegetable oil

4 carrots, peeled and chopped

½ yellow onion, chopped

½ green bell pepper, chopped

½ red bell pepper, chopped

5 garlic cloves

One 4 ½ pound (2 kg) chicken

Two 14.5 ounce (411 g) cans stewed tomatoes (Mexican style)

1 chicken bouillon cube

2 teaspoons cayenne

2 teaspoons kosher salt

2 teaspoons black pepper

1½ teaspoons chili powder

1½ teaspoons ground cumin

1½ teaspoons garlic powder

1½ teaspoons dried oregano

1½ teaspoons onion powder

1 teaspoon paprika

1 teaspoon red pepper flakes

TOPPINGS (OPTIONAL)

Homemade Tortilla Chips or strips (page 145)

3 green onions, chopped

3 limes, cut into wedges

Crema or sour cream

Avocado slices

Shredded cheese

Chopped fresh cilantro

HOMEMADE TORTILLA CHIPS

5 minutes
Prep time

15 minutes
Cook Time

20 minutes
Total Time

Level: ★☆☆☆

Makes 60

INGREDIENTS

10 small corn tortillas

Neutral oil, for frying

Kosher salt

TO BAKE THE TORTILLA CHIPS:

1. Preheat the oven to 350°F (180°C).

2. Cut each tortilla into six equal triangles.

3. Spread the triangles out in a single layer on baking sheets, and lightly brush with oil. Sprinkle with salt.

4. Bake for 12 to 15 minutes, until crispy and golden brown.

5. Remove from the oven and let cool for a few minutes before serving.

TO FRY THE TORTILLA CHIPS:

1. Cut each tortilla into six equal triangles or into strips.

2. In a skillet or deep fryer, heat enough oil to submerge the tortilla chips. Heat the oil to around 350°F (180°C).

3. Working in batches, add the tortilla chips to the oil and fry until golden brown and crispy, 2 to 3 minutes.

4. Use a slotted spoon or tongs to transfer the chips to a paper towel–lined plate.

5. Once the chips have cooled slightly, sprinkle with salt.

SPECIAL TOUCHES: You can make tortilla chips in any shape using corn tortillas and shape cutters!

CHUNKY GUACAMOLE

15 minutes
Prep time

0 minutes
Cook Time

15 minutes
Total Time

Level: ★☆☆☆

Makes 2 cups (480 g)

INGREDIENTS

4 ripe avocados

1 medium tomato, seeded and diced

½ small red onion, finely diced

1 jalapeño, seeded and finely chopped

2 garlic cloves, minced

¼ cup (4 g) chopped fresh cilantro

Juice of 1 lime

Kosher salt and black pepper

TOOLS

Molcajete

1. Halve the avocados, remove the pits, and scoop the flesh into a medium bowl.

2. Mash the avocado in a molcajete or bowl (using a fork) until it reaches your desired consistency.

3. Add the tomato, onion, jalapeño, garlic, and cilantro. Mix with a spoon.

4. Squeeze in the lime juice and stir well. Season with salt and pepper to taste.

5. Serve immediately or refrigerate until ready to serve.

TIP: To keep the guacamole from browning, I like to add a little more lime juice on the top layer and pack it into an airtight container for lunchtime. Don't forget to pack an ice pack to keep it cool.

GARLIC HERB STEAK + BROWN SUGAR BAKED SWEET POTATO

My girls love a good steak. This steak is seared to perfection and adorned with garlic, butter, and rosemary. For the sides, add a velvety brown sugar baked sweet potato, medley of berries, crispy cheese sticks, and marshmallows.

GARLIC HERB STEAK

30 minutes
Prep time

20 minutes
Cook Time

50 minutes
Total Time

Level: ★☆☆☆

Serves 4

INGREDIENTS

1 pound (454 g) sirloin, ribeye, or New York strip steak, 1 inch (2.5 cm) thick

Kosher salt and black pepper

2 tablespoons olive oil

2 garlic cloves, smashed

2 fresh rosemary sprigs

2 tablespoons butter

TOOLS

Cast-iron skillet

1. Let the steak sit at room temperature for about 30 minutes before cooking.

2. Preheat the oven to 400°F (200°C).

3. Season both sides of the steak generously with salt and pepper.

4. Heat a large cast-iron skillet over high heat. Add the olive oil, then add the steak and cook for 2 to 3 minutes without disturbing. Flip the steak and cook the other side until you get a nice sear, another 2 to 3 minutes.

5. Add the garlic, rosemary, and butter. Once the butter has melted, spoon it over the steak for about 2 minutes to baste.

6. Transfer the skillet to the oven and bake for 8 to 10 minutes, until the internal temperature of the steak reaches 135°F (60°C) for medium-rare or 145°F (63°C) for medium. (For lunches, I cook them a little longer: 2 to 3 minutes for medium well or 150°F/66°C.)

7. Remove the skillet from the oven and let the steak rest for 5 minutes before slicing and serving.

BROWN SUGAR BAKED SWEET POTATO

10 minutes
Prep time

1 hour
Cook Time

1 hour and 10 minutes
Total Time

Level: ★☆☆☆

Serves 4

INGREDIENTS

4 medium sweet potatoes

8 tablespoons unsalted butter

½ cup (100 g) brown sugar

1 teaspoon ground cinnamon

½ teaspoon kosher salt

TOOLS

Baking sheet

Parchment paper

1. Preheat the oven to 375°F (190°C). Line a baking sheet with parchment paper.

2. Pierce each sweet potato with a fork or knife in several places, then place on the baking sheet.

3. Bake for 45 to 50 minutes, until the potatoes are tender and can easily be pierced with a knife. Turn them once or twice so that they cook evenly.

4. Meanwhile, melt the butter in a small saucepan over low heat. Add the brown sugar, cinnamon, and salt, stirring until the sugar is dissolved.

5. Remove the sweet potatoes from the oven and let cool.

6. Use a sharp knife to slice the sweet potatoes lengthwise down the middle, but don't cut all the way through.

7. Pour the butter and brown sugar mixture over the potatoes, making sure to spread it evenly across the top and sides.

8. Return the sweet potatoes to the oven and bake for an additional 10 to 15 minutes, until the tops are caramelized and bubbly.

9. Remove from the oven and serve hot. Enjoy!

"Heaven" — **DJ Sammy, Yanou, Do**

"You miss 100 percent of the shots you don't take."

—WAYNE GRETZKY

MINI TURKEY POT PIES + FLOWER-SHAPED MAPLE CARROTS

This mini turkey pot pie is filled with tender turkey and veggies under a flaky crust. Pair with sweet, flower-shaped, glazed maple carrots. For some crunch, add Parmesan crisps. And for a sweet treat, of course, fill your lunch box with mini chocolate chip cookies, kiwi, and pomegranate seeds.

MINI TURKEY POT PIES

10 minutes
Prep time

35 minutes
Cook Time

45 minutes
Total Time

Level: ★★☆☆

Makes 4

1. Preheat your oven to 400°F (200°C). Grease four ramekins or small oven-safe bowls with butter.

2. In a large skillet over medium-high heat, add the butter and onions. Sauté the onions until tender, about 5 minutes. Add the flour and stir well to coat.

3. Gradually pour in the broth and milk, stirring continuously. Cook over medium heat until the mixture thickens and starts to bubble, 6 to 8 minutes.

4. Add the turkey and frozen vegetables to the skillet. Season with salt and pepper to taste. Stir well to combine.

5. Divide the mixture equally among the ramekins.

6. Cut each puff pastry sheet into four equal squares. Place one square of pastry on top of each ramekin, covering the turkey mixture.

7. Use a fork to press down the edges of the pastry, sealing it to the sides of the ramekins. Brush the tops of the pastry with the beaten egg to create a golden finish. Make a small slit on top of each pastry to allow steam to escape during baking.

8. Place the ramekins on a baking sheet and bake for 20 to 25 minutes, until the pastry is puffed up and golden brown.

9. Remove from the oven and let cool for a few minutes before serving.

TIP: For packed lunches, bake the puff pastries separately to add on top of the filling when it's time to eat.

INGREDIENTS

3 tablespoons butter, plus more for greasing

½ cup (80 g) chopped onion

¼ cup (30 g) all-purpose flour

1 cup (240 ml) chicken or turkey broth

½ cup (120 ml) milk

2 cups (280 g) diced cooked turkey

1 cup (150 g) frozen mixed vegetables (carrots, peas, corn)

Kosher salt and black pepper

2 sheets frozen puff pastry, thawed

1 egg, beaten

TOOLS

Four 8-ounce (240 ml) ramekins

Baking sheet

FLOWER-SHAPED MAPLE CARROTS

15 minutes
Prep time

15 minutes
Cook Time

30 minutes
Total Time

Level: ★★☆☆   **Serves 2 to 4**

INGREDIENTS

4 to 6 large carrots

2 tablespoons unsalted butter

Kosher salt and black pepper

2 tablespoons maple syrup

TOOLS

Vegetable peeler

1½ inch (3 cm) flower-shaped
food cutter

1. Peel the carrots and thinly slice them into ⅛-inch-thick (3 mm) rounds.

2. Using a flower-shaped cutter, cut flower shapes out of the carrots.

3. In a large skillet over medium heat, melt the butter. Add the carrots and season them with salt and pepper.

4. Cook, stirring occasionally, until tender and lightly browned, about 10 minutes.

5. Drizzle the maple syrup over the carrots and stir to coat. Continue cooking, stirring frequently, until the carrots are caramelized and glazed, around 5 minutes more.

6. Remove from the heat and serve!

TIP: Use the leftover carrot pieces to make Vegetable Stock (page 259) or Chicken Stock (page 260).

"Lovely Day" — **Bill Withers**

Be the reason someone smiles today.

BLACKENED SALMON + CAESAR SALAD

This blackened salmon is perfectly seared and coated with a savory blend of spices; it's served on a bed of classic Caesar salad, with crisp romaine lettuce tossed in a creamy dressing, then topped with shaved Parmesan and garlic croutons. Enjoy a side of juicy corn on the cob with butter and heart-shaped strawberries to add a touch of love to anyone's lunch.

BLACKENED SALMON

10 minutes
Prep time

10 minutes
Cook Time

20 minutes
Total Time

| Level: ★★☆☆ | Serves 4 to 6 |

1. In a small bowl, combine the paprika, thyme, oregano, garlic powder, onion powder, Old Bay, salt, black pepper, and cayenne.

2. Pat the salmon dry with a paper towel to remove any excess moisture.

3. Rub the spice mixture evenly onto both sides of the salmon filets.

4. Heat a skillet or a cast-iron pan over medium-high heat. Melt the butter, then carefully place the salmon, skin-side down, into the pan.

5. Cook the salmon until it reaches your desired level of doneness, 4 to 5 minutes on each side (cooking time may vary depending on the thickness of your filets). The salmon should be opaque and easily flake with a fork when cooked through.

6. Remove the salmon from the heat and let it rest for a few minutes. Serve with lemons on the side.

INGREDIENTS

1 tablespoon paprika

1½ teaspoons dried thyme

1½ teaspoons dried oregano

1 teaspoon garlic powder

1 teaspoon onion powder

1 teaspoon Old Bay

1 teaspoon kosher salt

½ teaspoon black pepper

½ teaspoon cayenne, or to taste

Four 6 to 8-ounce (170 to 225 g) skin-on salmon filets, pin bones removed

2 tablespoons butter or olive oil

Lemon wedges, for serving

CAESAR SALAD

10 minutes
Prep time

0 minutes
Cook Time

10 minutes
Total Time

Level: ★☆☆☆

Serves 4

1. To a large bowl, add the lettuce. Pour in the Caesar dressing (start with ¼ cup (60 ml) and add more as desired).

2. Toss the lettuce with the dressing until it is evenly coated.

3. Add the Parmesan and toss again to distribute it throughout the salad.

4. Season with salt and pepper to taste.

5. Add the croutons and toss everything together one final time. Serve with lemon wedges.

NOTE: I like to pack the dressing and toppings separately for lunch to keep them from getting soggy.

INGREDIENTS

1 large head romaine lettuce, torn into bite-size pieces

½ cup (120 ml) Caesar dressing

⅓ cup (30 g) grated Parmesan

Kosher salt and black pepper, to taste

½ cup (20 g) Crunchy Garlic Croutons (page 135)

Lemon wedges, for serving

BUTTERY DILL SALMON + CREAMY CUCUMBER SALAD

Savor the irresistible flavors of this delicious salmon, cooked to perfection with a rich and buttery glaze. Pair it with a creamy cucumber salad, with crunchy cucumbers coated in a velvety dressing. To complete the lunch, add some steamed broccoli.

BUTTERY DILL SALMON ⋮

5 minutes
Prep time

20 minutes
Cook Time

25 minutes
Total Time

Level: ★☆☆☆

Serves 4

INGREDIENTS ✕

Four 5-ounce (142 g) skin-on salmon filets

4 tablespoons unsalted butter, at room temperature

2 tablespoons chopped fresh dill

Kosher salt and black pepper

½ yellow onion, thinly sliced

1 lemon, sliced

FOR SERVING

Cooked white rice

Lemon wedges, optional

TOOLS

Baking sheet

Parchment paper

1. Preheat your oven to 400°F (200°C). Line a baking sheet with aluminium foil.

2. Place the salmon on the baking sheet, skin-side down.

3. In a small bowl, mix the butter and dill. Season with salt and pepper to taste.

4. Spread the mixture evenly over the salmon filets, making sure they are well coated. Lay the onion and lemon slices on top of the salmon. Cover with aluminium foil.

5. Bake for 15 to 20 minutes, removing the foil for the last 5 minutes, until the salmon is cooked through and flakes easily with a fork.

6. Remove the salmon from the oven and let it rest for a few minutes.

7. Serve hot over a bed of rice, garnished with lemon wedges, if desired. Let it cool before packing into a lunch.

CREAMY CUCUMBER SALAD ⋮

10 minutes
Prep time

0 minutes
Cook Time

40 minutes
with chill time
Total Time

Level: ★☆☆☆

Serves 4

INGREDIENTS ✕

½ cup (120 ml) sour cream

¼ cup (60 ml) mayonnaise

2 tablespoons chopped fresh dill

1 tablespoon white vinegar

1 teaspoon sugar

Kosher salt and black pepper

2 large cucumbers, thinly sliced

TOOLS

Plastic wrap

1. In a medium bowl, combine the sour cream, mayonnaise, dill, vinegar, sugar, and salt and pepper to taste. Stir well.

2. Add the cucumbers and toss gently to coat.

3. Cover the bowl with plastic wrap and refrigerate for at least 30 minutes to allow the cucumber slices to marinate.

4. Before serving, give the salad a good stir to redistribute the dressing and coat the cucumbers evenly. Adjust the seasoning, if desired.

5. Serve chilled.

VEGGIE BURRITO BOWL + CILANTRO LIME RICE + AVOCADO CILANTRO DRESSING

This burrito bowl is packed with layers of flavor. Cilantro lime rice provides a fragrant and zesty foundation. On top of the rice, add sautéed bell peppers and onions, black beans, and corn. Serve with avocado dressing, lettuce and tomatoes, tortilla strips, and limes on the side for a satisfying and vibrant meal.

◄◄ ►II ►►

"Sunday Morning" — **No Doubt**

VEGGIE BURRITO BOWL

10 minutes Prep time

10 minutes Cook Time

20 minutes Total Time

Level: ★☆☆☆

Serves 2

1. In a large skillet, heat the oil over medium heat. Add the bell pepper and onion and cook until softened, about 5 minutes.

2. Add the beans, corn, chili powder, cumin, paprika, garlic powder, onion powder, salt, and pepper. Stir to combine and cook for another 3 to 4 minutes to allow the flavors to meld.

3. Divide the rice among bowls. Top with the black bean and corn mixture, diced tomatoes, sliced avocado, and any other desired toppings.

4. Squeeze lime juice over everything or add lime wedges on the side. Serve immediately and enjoy!

NOTES: When packing this lunch, I like to add the toppings on the side so they stay fresh. Feel free to add your favorite protein to this burrito bowl!

INGREDIENTS

2 tablespoons avocado oil

1 bell pepper, diced

½ small onion, diced

1 cup (240 g) drained and rinsed canned black beans

1 cup (160 g) corn kernels (fresh or canned)

1 teaspoon chili powder

½ teaspoon ground cumin

½ teaspoon paprika

¼ teaspoon garlic powder

¼ teaspoon onion powder

Kosher salt and black pepper

1 cup (195 g) Cilantro Lime Rice (page 161)

1 roma tomato, diced

1 avocado, sliced

Juice of 1 lime

TOPPINGS (OPTIONAL)

Avocado Cilantro Dressing (page 161)

Sour cream

Shredded cheese

Salsa

Guacamole

Shredded lettuce

Lime wedges

CILANTRO LIME RICE

5 minutes
Prep time

25 minutes
Cook Time

30 minutes
Total Time

Level: ★☆☆☆

Serves 4

INGREDIENTS

1 cup (185 g) long-grain white rice

½ teaspoon kosher salt, or to taste

Juice of 1 lime (about 2 tablespoons)

2 tablespoons chopped fresh cilantro

1. Rinse the rice under cold water to remove excess starch. Drain well.

2. In a medium saucepan, bring 2 cups (480 ml) of water to a boil. Add the rice and salt, stir, and reduce the heat to low.

3. Cover the saucepan with a tight-fitting lid and simmer until the rice is tender and the liquid has been absorbed, 15 to 20 minutes.

4. Remove the pan from the heat and let sit, covered, for an additional 5 minutes to steam.

5. In a small bowl, combine the lime juice and cilantro.

6. Fluff the rice with a fork, then pour in the lime juice and cilantro mixture. Gently toss to evenly distribute the flavors.

7. Taste and adjust the salt if necessary.

AVOCADO CILANTRO DRESSING

10 minutes
Prep time

30 minutes
Cook Time

40 minutes
Total Time

Level: ★☆☆☆

Makes 1 cup (240 ml)

INGREDIENTS

1 ripe avocado

¼ cup (60 ml) plain Greek yogurt

Juice of 1 lime (about 2 tablespoons)

3 tablespoons extra virgin olive oil

3 tablespoons chopped fresh cilantro

1 garlic clove, minced

Kosher salt and black pepper

TOOLS

Blender or food processor

1. Halve the avocado, remove the pit, and scoop the flesh into a blender or food processor.

2. Add the yogurt, lime juice, olive oil, cilantro, garlic, and salt and pepper to taste.

3. Blend until smooth and creamy. If the dressing is too thick, add water, 1 tablespoon at a time, until you reach your desired consistency.

4. Transfer the dressing to a jar or container, cover, and refrigerate for at least 30 minutes to allow the flavors to meld.

5. Serve the dressing drizzled over salads, as a dip for vegetables, or as a sauce for tacos or burrito bowls.

TIP: Always taste as you go.

"You are my favorite everything."

"Chemtrails Over the Country Club"
— **Lana Del Rey**

BEEF & MUSHROOM STROGANOFF + PICKLED BEET & GOAT CHEESE SALAD

Stroganoff is such a classic dish. Tender beef and earthy mushrooms are cooked to perfection in a creamy sauce, creating a comforting experience with every bite. In this salad, the tanginess of pickled beets perfectly complements the creamy goat cheese. Serve with juicy raspberries to bring a burst of freshness to the palate.

BEEF & MUSHROOM STROGANOFF

10 minutes
Prep time

20 minutes
Cook Time

30 minutes
Total Time

Level: ★★☆☆

Serves 4

1. Cook the noodles according to package directions until al dente. Drain and rinse under cold water to cool. Set aside.
2. In a large skillet, heat the butter and oil over medium-high heat.
3. Add the beef and cook until browned, 2 to 3 minutes per side. Remove from the skillet and set aside.
4. To the same skillet, add the mushrooms, onion, and garlic. Cook until the mushrooms have released their liquid and the onions are softened, 5 to 6 minutes.
5. Return the beef to the skillet. Stir in the broth and Worcestershire sauce.
6. Reduce the heat to low and simmer until the sauce has thickened slightly, 5 to 10 minutes. Season with salt and pepper to taste.
7. Serve the stroganoff over the noodles. Garnish with a dollop of sour cream and fresh parsley.

INGREDIENTS

1 pound (454 g) egg noodles

2 tablespoons butter

1 tablespoon olive oil

1 pound (450 g) beef sirloin, thinly sliced

8 ounces (225 g) cremini mushrooms, sliced

1 medium onion, finely chopped

3 garlic cloves, minced

1 cup (240 ml) beef broth

1 teaspoon Worcestershire sauce

Kosher salt and black pepper

Sour cream

Chopped fresh parsley

PICKLED BEET & GOAT CHEESE SALAD

10 minutes
Prep time

0 minutes
Cook Time

10 minutes
Total Time

Level: ★★☆☆

Serves 4

1. In a large bowl, combine the greens, beets, cheese, corn, and black olives.

2. Make the dressing: In a small bowl, whisk the olive oil, vinegar, salt, and pepper until well combined.

3. Pour the dressing over the salad and toss gently to coat.

4. Serve immediately!

TIP: Pack the dressing separately for lunches and meal preps.

INGREDIENTS

4 cups (140 g) mixed greens

1 cup (225 g) sliced pickled baby beets

½ cup (120 g) crumbled goat cheese

½ cup (80 g) drained canned corn

3 tablespoons sliced black olives

DRESSING

2 tablespoons olive oil

2 tablespoon balsamic vinegar

Kosher salt and pepper

HEART-SHAPED CRAB CAKES + SWEET & SOUR DIPPING SAUCE

Fall in love with these heart-shaped crab cakes, a perfect blend of succulent crab meat and flavorful seasonings, paired with a sweet and sour dipping sauce. Pair with lightly steamed green beans, which offer a fresh and nutritious balance to the richness of the crab cakes. Star-cut grapes and confetti popcorn add a festive twist.

HEART–SHAPED CRAB CAKES

15 minutes
Prep time

12 minutes
Cook Time

27 minutes
Total Time

Level: ★★★☆

Makes 8

INGREDIENTS

Nonstick cooking spray

1 pound (454 g) fresh lump crabmeat

2 tablespoons mayonnaise

1 teaspoon Dijon mustard

1 teaspoon Worcestershire sauce

1 egg

2 garlic cloves, minced

¼ cup (30 g) finely chopped red bell pepper

¼ cup (25 g) panko bread crumbs

Kosher salt and black pepper

TOOLS

Baking sheet

Heart-shaped cookie cutter, optional

1. Preheat your oven to 375°F (190°C). Lightly coat a baking sheet with cooking spray.

2. In a large bowl, combine the crab, mayonnaise, mustard, Worcestershire sauce, egg, garlic, bell pepper, panko, salt, and black pepper.

3. Divide the crab mixture into eight equal portions and shape each one into a heart shape with your hands (you can also use a heart-shaped cookie cutter). Place the crab cakes on the baking sheet.

4. Bake for 10 to 12 minutes, until golden brown on top and heated through.

5. Serve hot with sweet and sour sauce.

SWEET & SOUR DIPPING SAUCE

5 minutes
Prep time

10 minutes
Cook Time

15 minutes
Total Time

Level: ★☆☆☆

Makes 1 cup (240 ml)

INGREDIENTS

½ cup (120 ml) white vinegar

½ cup (100 g) sugar

¼ cup (60 ml) ketchup

1 tablespoon soy sauce

1 teaspoon garlic powder

1 teaspoon onion powder

2 tablespoons cornstarch

1. In a medium saucepan, combine the vinegar, sugar, ketchup, soy sauce, garlic powder, and onion powder. Stir until the sugar has dissolved, 2 to 3 minutes.

2. Bring to a boil over medium-high heat.

3. While the mixture is heating up, mix the cornstarch and 2 tablespoons cold water in a small bowl to create a slurry.

4. Once the sauce mixture is boiling, reduce the heat to medium-low and pour in the cornstarch slurry, whisking constantly.

5. Continue whisking until it has thickened to your desired consistency, 1 to 2 minutes.

6. Remove from the heat and let cool to room temperature before serving.

AROUND THE WORLD

Be the person your dog thinks you are.

"Cruisin'" — **Huey Lewis & Gwyneth Paltrow**

HAWAII:
SPAM MUSUBI +
MAC SALAD +
PICKLED MANGOES

This mouthwatering Hawaiian lunch pairs the iconic Spam musubi with flavorful mac salad, tangy pickled mangoes, and chocolate-dipped dried pineapples. Complete the meal with heart-shaped peach gummies and crispy banana chips for a taste of the tropics, which will transport you to the blissful shores of Hawaii.

SPAM MUSUBI

15 minutes
Prep time

10 minutes
Cook Time

25 minutes
Total Time

Level: ★☆☆☆

Serves 4

1. Slice the Spam into eight ¼-inch-thick (6 mm) pieces.

2. In a small bowl, mix the soy sauce, oyster sauce, and brown sugar.

3. Heat a large nonstick pan over medium heat and add the Spam. Cook until browned and slightly crispy, 2 to 4 minutes on each side.

4. Use scissors to cut the nori seaweed into four equal rectangles.

5. Pour the sauce mixture onto the Spam, flipping to coat, and cook for 1 more minute or until the sauce thickens and coats the Spam evenly. Remove from the heat and set aside.

6. Place a sheet of nori on a flat surface and place the musubi mold in the center.

7. Scoop about ¼ cup (50 g) of rice into the mold and press down firmly to form a solid layer.

8. Add a slice of Spam on top of the rice, then scoop another ¼ cup (50 g) of sushi rice over the Spam and press down again.

9. Wrap the nori sheet around the rice and Spam tightly, like a present, seam side down.

10. Repeat steps 5 to 8 with the remaining ingredients.

11. Slice each Spam musubi into bite-size pieces and serve warm or at room temperature.

INGREDIENTS

One 12-ounce (340 g) can Spam

1½ tablespoons soy sauce

1½ tablespoons oyster sauce

1½ tablespoons brown sugar

4 sheets nori seaweed

4 cups (800 g) cooked sushi rice, room temperature

TOOLS

Scissors

Musubi mold

TUNA MAC SALAD

20 minutes
Prep time

25 minutes
Cook Time

45 minutes
Total Time

Level: ★☆☆☆

Serves 8

INGREDIENTS

2 small Yukon gold or red potatoes, cubed

Kosher salt and black pepper

1 pound (454 g) elbow macaroni

2 cups (480 ml) mayonnaise

3 tablespoons milk

1 tablespoon sugar or honey

1½ teaspoons apple cider vinegar

1½ teaspoons rice vinegar

One 5-ounce (142 g) can tuna in water, drained

1 cup (110 g) shredded carrots

1 cup (120 g) finely diced celery

½ cup (55 g) diced onion

1. Place the potatoes in a small pot of salted water and bring to a boil. Cook the potatoes until they are tender but not mushy, 10 to 15 minutes. Drain and set aside.

2. While the potatoes are cooking, cook the macaroni according to the package instructions. Drain and set aside.

3. In a large bowl, combine the mayonnaise, milk, sugar, apple cider vinegar, rice vinegar, 1 teaspoon salt, and ½ teaspoon pepper. Stir well to combine.

4. Add the tuna, macaroni, potatoes, carrots, celery, and onions to the bowl. Stir well. Taste and add salt and pepper as needed.

5. Serve warm or cover the bowl with plastic wrap and refrigerate for a few hours before serving.

PICKLED MANGOES

10 minutes
Prep time

5 minutes
Cook Time

24 hours
with chilling time
Total Time

Level: ★☆☆☆

Makes two 1-pint (475 ml) jars

INGREDIENTS

1 cup (240 ml) rice vinegar

½ cup (100 g) sugar

1 tablespoon li hing mui powder (see Note)

1 teaspoon kosher salt

1 to 2 large green (unripe) mangoes, peeled and sliced lengthwise into thin strips

TOOLS

Two 1-pint (475 ml) jars

1. In a small saucepan, combine the vinegar, sugar, li hing mui powder, and salt. Heat over medium heat until the sugar dissolves, 3 to 5 minutes, stirring occasionally.

2. Place the mangoes into clean glass jars.

3. Pour the vinegar mixture over the mangoes, ensuring that they are completely submerged.

4. Let the mixture cool to room temperature, then cover the jar with a lid or plastic wrap.

5. Refrigerate for at least 24 hours before serving to allow the flavors to develop.

6. Serve as a tangy and sweet condiment or snack.

NOTE: Li hing mui powder is a popular Hawaiian seasoning made from dried plum or apricot, which is then mixed with various spices and preserved in a tangy, salty-sweet powder. It's a versatile ingredient to sprinkle on fruits, candies, or popcorn, or to incorporate into cocktails and desserts.

You are the greatest gift I have ever received.

000

HAWAII:

BUTTERY GARLIC SHRIMP + SHOYU AHI TUNA POKE

This is one of my favorite meals to eat in Hawaii: buttery garlic shrimp, like the ones you can get at a shrimp truck in North Shore, and shoyu ahi tuna poke. Accompanied by sides of mango, dragon fruit, and banana chips, this meal will transport your taste buds to the tropical islands. The rich, savory shrimp and the fresh, marinated tuna are a truly Hawaiian experience.

◀◀　▶ǁ　▶▶

"Cruel to Be Kind" — **Letters to Cleo**

BUTTERY GARLIC SHRIMP

5 minutes
Prep time

10 minutes
Cook Time

15 minutes
Total Time

Level: ★★☆☆

Serves 4

INGREDIENTS

4 tablespoons butter

4 garlic cloves, minced

¼ teaspoon red pepper flakes, optional

1 pound (454 g) large shrimp, shells on

Kosher salt and black pepper

2 tablespoons lemon juice

Chopped fresh parsley

Lemon wedges, for serving

1. In a large skillet, melt the butter over medium heat. Add the garlic and red pepper flakes, if using. Cook until fragrant, about 1 minute.

2. Increase the heat to medium-high and add the shrimp. Season with salt and pepper. Cook until the shrimp are pink and opaque, 2 to 3 minutes on each side.

3. Pour the lemon juice over the shrimp and toss until well coated, 1 to 2 minutes.

4. Remove the skillet from the heat and top with parsley.

5. Serve with lemon wedges on the side.

TIP: When packing this for your little ones, peel the shrimp to make them easier and cleaner to eat.

SHOYU AHI TUNA POKE

10 minutes
Prep time

0 minutes
Cook Time

10 minutes
Total Time

Level: ★☆☆☆

Serves 2 to 4

INGREDIENTS

1 pound (454 g) fresh sashimi-grade ahi tuna steak, chilled and cut into ½-inch (1 cm) cubes

¼ cup (60 ml) soy sauce

1 tablespoon rice vinegar

2 tablespoons sesame oil

¼ cup (25 g) thinly sliced Maui or yellow onion

¼ cup (15 g) chopped green onions, plus more for garnish

1½ teaspoons sugar

½ teaspoon gochugaru (Korean red chili pepper flakes), optional

FOR SERVING (OPTIONAL)

Nori flakes

Toasted sesame seeds

Cooked sushi rice

1. In a large bowl, combine the tuna, soy sauce, rice vinegar, sesame oil, onion, green onions, sugar, and gochugaru, if desired.

2. Gently toss with your hands or a spoon. Adjust the seasoning and top with nori, sesame seeds, and green onion. Serve with rice, if desired.

NOTE: Add sriracha to make it spicier!

INDONESIA:
SATE AYAM CHICKEN SKEWERS + PEANUT SAUCE + KLEPON

Immerse yourself in the captivating flavors of Indonesia with succulent sate ayam chicken skewers, accompanied by a tangy peanut sauce, refreshing cucumber slices, and juicy tomatoes. Conclude your culinary adventure with klepon, sweet pandan rice cakes that are a decadent delight. Olive, my youngest, is part Indonesian and would love to share this culinary journey with you!

PEANUT SAUCE

10 minutes
Prep time

15 minutes
Cook Time

25 minutes
Total Time

| Level: ★☆☆☆ | Makes: 1 cup (240 ml) |

INGREDIENTS

1 cup (146 g) unsalted roasted peanuts

1 tablespoon vegetable oil

1 shallot, minced

2 garlic cloves, minced

1 teaspoon ground coriander

1 teaspoon ground cumin

½ teaspoon red pepper flakes, or to taste

2 tablespoons kecap manis (Indonesian sweet soy sauce)

1 tablespoon tamarind paste

½ teaspoon kosher salt

1. In a blender or food processor, grind the peanuts to form a coarse powder. Set aside.

2. In a small pan, heat the oil over medium heat. Add the shallot and garlic, and cook until fragrant and golden brown, 1 to 2 minutes

3. Add the coriander, cumin, and red pepper flakes to the pan, and stir for about a minute to toast the spices.

4. Add the ground peanuts, kecap manis, tamarind paste, salt, and 1 cup (240 ml) water to the pan. Stir well to combine all the ingredients.

5. Reduce the heat to low and simmer for 10 to 15 minutes, stirring occasionally, until thickened. If the sauce is too thick, you can add a little more water. Remove from the heat and let cool before serving.

6. Serve alongside grilled chicken satays, drizzled on salads, or with spring rolls. Store in an airtight container in the fridge for up to a week.

SATE AYAM CHICKEN SKEWERS

1 hour
Prep time

15 minutes
Cook Time

1 hour and 15 minutes
Total Time

| Level: ★★★☆ | Serves 4 |

1. Make the marinade: In a large bowl, combine the soy sauce, brown sugar, kecap manis, vegetable oil, garlic, lime juice, coriander, cumin, turmeric, and chili powder, if using. Mix well.

2. Add the chicken to the marinade and toss to coat. Let marinate for at least 1 hour or overnight in the refrigerator.

3. Preheat the oven at 400°F (200°C). Line a baking sheet with parchment paper.

4. Thread 4 to 5 chicken cubes onto each bamboo skewer. Place the skewers onto the baking sheet.

5. Bake for 10 to 12 minutes, until the chicken is cooked through and slightly charred. Flip the skewers halfway through and baste them with the remaining marinade.

6. Turn the broiler on high and broil for 1 to 2 minutes, until nicely charred. Keep an eye on them!

7. Serve hot with peanut sauce, cucumber and tomato slices, and warm steamed rice.

INGREDIENTS

3 tablespoons soy sauce

2 tablespoons brown sugar

2 tablespoons kecap manis (Indonesian sweet soy sauce)

2 tablespoons vegetable oil

2 garlic cloves, minced

1 tablespoon lime juice

1 teaspoon ground coriander

1 teaspoon ground cumin

1 teaspoon ground turmeric

1 teaspoon chili powder, optional

1 pound (454 g) boneless chicken thighs, cubed

FOR SERVING

Peanut Sauce (page 179)

Cucumber slices

Tomato slices

Steamed rice

TOOLS

Bamboo skewers, soaked in water for at least 30 minutes

Baking sheet

Parchment paper

KLEPON

(SWEET PANDAN RICE CAKES)

15 minutes
Prep time

25 minutes
Cook Time

40 minutes
Total Time

Level: ★★★☆	Makes 10 to 12

1. In a large bowl, combine the rice flour, 1 cup (240 ml) room temperature water, pandan flavoring, and salt. Mix well to form a soft dough. Adjust the consistency by adding more rice flour or water if needed.

2. Take a small portion, about 1 to 2 tablespoonfuls, of the dough and flatten it in your hand. Place a cube of palm sugar in the center and carefully seal the edges to form a ball. Roll it between your hands to make it smooth and even. Repeat with the remaining dough.

3. Fill a medium pot halfway with water and bring to a boil. Carefully drop the klepon balls into the water, in batches if necessary, and cook until they float to the surface, 5 to 7 minutes. Make sure not to overcrowd the pot, so the klepon don't stick together.

4. Place the shredded coconut in a shallow bowl.

5. Using a slotted spoon, remove the klepon from the boiling water and transfer them directly into the bowl of coconut. Roll them around to coat each ball evenly.

6. Serve immediately and enjoy!

NOTE: Klepon are best eaten on the same day they are made. Store any leftovers in an airtight container at room temperature for a few days, but they may harden over time.

INGREDIENTS

2 cups (250 g) glutinous rice flour

1 teaspoon pandan flavoring

Pinch of kosher salt

¼ cup (100 g) palm sugar or gula melaka, cut into tiny cubes

1 cup (85 g) sweetened shredded coconut

KOREA:
KIMBAP ROLLS + GYERAN MARI + OI-SOBAGI

This Korean lunch features kimbap rolls—fresh and vibrant ingredients encased in seaweed—a lunch my mom used to lovingly pack for me during my childhood. Accompanying the rolls is gyeran mari, a beautifully rolled omelet, and oi sobagi, a stuffed cucumber kimchi that provides a harmonious blend of spice and crunch as a side dish. Serve with Korean melon (with edible seeds), pomegranate seeds, and mango marshmallows, for snacking pleasure.

KIMBAP ROLLS

20 minutes
Prep time

15 minutes
Cook Time

35 minutes
Total Time

| Level: ★★☆☆ | Makes 4 |

INGREDIENTS

2 small carrots, julienned

3 tablespoons sesame oil, divided

Kosher salt and black pepper

2 cups (60 g) spinach

1½ cup (180 g) julienned burdock root

1½ teaspoons soy sauce, plus more for serving

1½ teaspoons sugar

2 cups (400 g) cooked sushi rice

2 tablespoons rice vinegar

Nori seaweed sheets

1 cucumber, julienned

5 ounces (142 g) pickled daikon (danmuji), julienned

TOOLS

Bamboo sushi mat

1. In a medium pan, sauté the carrots in 1½ teaspoons of sesame oil until tender, about 5 minutes. Season with salt and pepper to taste.

2. In a medium pot, bring 3 cups (720 ml) of water to a boil. Add the spinach and blanch for 30 to 60 seconds. Transfer to a bowl with ice water to cool for about 2 minutes. Drain and squeeze out the excess water, then salt and pepper to taste.

3. In the same pan, sauté the burdock root in 1½ teaspoons of sesame oil over medium heat. Add the soy sauce and sugar and cook until the burdock root is tender, 4 to 5 minutes.

4. Transfer the rice to a large bowl and pour in the vinegar. Mix gently to coat, then let cool completely.

5. Place a sheet of nori, shiny side down, on a clean surface. Take a handful of sushi rice, using a rice scooper, and spread it evenly over the bottom third of the nori sheet, leaving a small border at the bottom.

6. Arrange three to five strips of each filling ingredient (cucumber, carrots, spinach, burdock root, and pickled daikon) in a line on top of the rice.

7. Carefully roll the nori sheet tightly, starting from the bottom, using your hands or a sushi mat to help. Apply a little bit of water or rice on the edge of the nori to seal the roll.

8. Repeat steps 5 to 7 with the remaining nori sheets and fillings.

9. Cut into ½-inch-thick (1 cm) slices. Serve with soy sauce for dipping.

GYERAN MARI
(ROLLED OMELET)

5 minutes
Prep time

10 minutes
Cook Time

15 minutes
Total Time

Level: ★★☆☆

Makes 1

INGREDIENTS

3 eggs

1½ tablespoons finely diced carrots

1½ tablespoons finely chopped
green onions

Kosher salt and black pepper

Vegetable oil

TOOLS

Nonstick rectangular omelet pan

1. In a medium bowl, whisk the eggs, then whisk in the carrots, green onions, and salt and pepper to taste.

2. Heat a nonstick rectangular omelet pan or medium nonstick frying pan over medium heat and lightly coat with oil.

3. Pour half of the egg mixture into the pan and quickly spread it out evenly. Cook until the edges start to set, about 1 minute.

4. Using a rubber spatula, lift one end of the cooked egg (about 1½ inches/4 cm) and fold it over to the other side, creating a small, folded portion at one end.

5. Reduce the heat and continue to cook the omelet, gently folding and rolling it from one end to the other with the spatula as it cooks. If needed, add a little more oil to the pan to prevent sticking.

6. Pull the folded part to one side and add the other half of the raw egg mixture to the other side, keeping the heat on low.

7. Cook until lightly golden on all sides, then remove from the heat and let cool slightly. Slice crosswise into bite-size pieces and serve as a side dish or snack.

OI–SOBAGI
(CUCUMBER KIMCHI)

30 minutes
Prep time

0 minutes
Cook Time

1 to 2 days
(including fermentation)
Total Time

Level: ★★☆☆	Serves 3 to 4

1. Cut off the ends of the cucumbers and slice them twice lengthwise, forming an X, leaving ½ inch (1 cm) from one end so the cucumber is still connected.

2. Transfer to a large bowl, sprinkle with salt, and toss to coat. Let sit for about 30 minutes to draw out excess moisture.

3. Meanwhile, combine the garlic, ginger, gochugaru, fish sauce, sugar, and ¼ cup (60 ml) water in a small bowl. Mix well to combine. Add the carrots, onion, and chives. Mix once more to incorporate.

4. Rinse the cucumbers under cold running water to remove excess salt. Gently squeeze to remove any remaining water.

5. Stuff the cucumber pockets with the prepared seasoning paste and ensure that each cucumber is coated evenly.

6. Transfer to a clean, airtight container or jar and press down firmly to remove any air bubbles.

7. You can eat this right away, but allowing the cucumber kimchi to ferment at room temperature for 1 to 2 days is best. The cucumbers will become slightly pickled.

8. Taste the kimchi. Once it's reached the desired level of fermentation, transfer to the refrigerator to slow down the fermentation process.

9. Serve chilled as a side dish. Store in the refrigerator for up to several weeks. The longer it ferments, the more complex and tangier the flavors become.

NOTE: During the fermentation process, you can expect to see a few changes. As the process begins, you may notice small bubbles forming. This is a sign that the beneficial bacteria present in the kimchi are actively fermenting the ingredients. Fermentation also produces a characteristic tangy and slightly sour smell. This aroma will become more pronounced as the kimchi ferments. The kimchi-making process can vary depending on several factors, such as temperature and personal preference, so it's a good idea to taste the kimchi along the way to determine when it has reached your desired level of fermentation.

INGREDIENTS

6 to 7 Persian cucumbers

2 tablespoons kosher salt

3 garlic cloves, minced

½ tablespoon grated ginger

2½ tablespoons gochugaru (Korean red pepper flakes)

¼ cup (60 ml) fish sauce

2 tablespoons sugar

½ cup (60 g) thinly sliced carrots

¼ cup (30 g) thinly sliced onion

½ cup (24 g) chopped chives

TOOLS

Airtight container or jar

Disposable gloves

"Candy" — **H.O.T.**

KOREA:

ROSE-SHAPED DUMPLINGS + DUMPLING DIPPING SAUCE + DALGONA CANDY

Transport your taste buds to Korea with rose-shaped dumplings (mandu) and a savory dipping sauce. These exquisitely crafted dumplings are shaped like delicate roses, offering a touch of elegance to any dining experience. The filling, a cherished recipe from my umma, holds a special place in my heart. Adding to the experience is dalgona candy, a fond childhood memory from my visits to Korea during summer breaks. This airy confection with its rich caramel flavor is a true delight, complemented by star-shaped chocolates.

ROSE-SHAPED DUMPLINGS

1 hour
Prep time

40 minutes
Cook Time

1 hour and 40 minutes
Total Time

Level: ★★★☆

Makes 16 to 18

1. In a large bowl, combine the beef, pork, cabbage, noodles, tofu, sprouts, chives, egg yolk, onion, garlic, ginger, sesame oil, soy sauce, sesame oil, salt, pepper and beef dasida. Mix well.

2. Place a sheet of parchment paper on a cutting board. Arrange four dumpling wrappers in a horizontal line, slightly overlapping, and brush a small amount of water in between the wrappers to secure them.

3. Use food coloring to brush a line about ½-inch (1 cm) thick across the tops and bottoms of the wrappers.

4. Spread about 2 tablespoons of filling in a horizontal line across the center of the wrappers leaving about ¾-inch (2 cm) of space on each end. Set out ½ cup (120 ml) of water. Wearing disposable gloves, dip your finger in the water, then run it along the edges of the wrappers.

5. Fold the wrappers in half lengthwise, from the bottom to the top. Seal all the edges with water. Starting at the left end, roll the wrappers to the other end. Use water to seal the edges.

6. Repeat steps 2 to 5 with the remaining dumpling wrappers and filling mixture, changing the parchment paper and replenishing the food coloring as needed.

7. Fill a large pot with about 2 inches (5 cm) of water and place a bamboo steamer basket lined with a piece of perforated parchment paper inside. Make sure the water level is below the steamer.

8. Working in batches, place the dumplings in the steamer basket, leaving an inch (2.5 cm) of space between each dumpling to prevent them from sticking together.

9. Bring the water to a boil over high heat, then reduce the heat to medium-low to maintain a steady steam. Cover and steam until the wrappers are translucent, the filling is cooked through, and a toothpick comes out clean, 30 to 40 minutes.

10. Use tongs to remove the dumplings. Serve immediately.

NOTE: You can freeze uncooked dumplings for up to 2 months. Line them up on a baking sheet lined with parchment paper and put them in the freezer for a couple of hours. Transfer to a plastic bag and store in the freezer. Thaw on your counter for 15 to 20 minutes, then start with step 7.

INGREDIENTS

⅓ pound (150 g) ground beef

⅓ pound (150 g) ground pork

3 leaves Napa cabbage, blanched and chopped

¾ cup (115 g) chopped cooked vermicelli noodles

3 ounces (85 g) firm tofu, drained and finely chopped

⅓ cup (60 g) chopped blanched mung bean sprouts

⅓ cup (15 g) chopped chives

1 egg yolk

2 tablespoons chopped yellow onion

2 tablespoons minced garlic

1½ tablespoons minced ginger

1 tablespoon sesame seeds

1 tablespoon soy sauce

2 teaspoons sesame oil

1½ teaspoons kosher salt

1 teaspoon black pepper

1 teaspoon beef dasida or beef bouillon

60 to 70 thin round dumpling wrappers

4 drops red food coloring or 2 teaspoons red beet powder and 2 tablespoons water

TOOLS

Parchment paper

Small brush

Disposable gloves

Perforated parchment paper circles

DUMPLING DIPPING SAUCE

10 minutes
Prep time

0 minutes
Cook Time

10 minutes
Total Time

Level: ★☆☆☆

Makes about ⅓ cup (80 ml)

INGREDIENTS

3 tablespoons soy sauce

1 tablespoon rice vinegar

2 garlic cloves, minced

1½ teaspoons sesame oil

1 teaspoon honey or sugar

1 teaspoon sesame seeds

1 green onion, finely chopped

1½ teaspoons finely diced jalapeño

1 teaspoon gochugaru, optional

1. In a small bowl, whisk together the soy sauce, vinegar, garlic, sesame oil, honey, and sesame seeds until well combined.

2. Taste the sauce and adjust the sweetness, acidity, and saltiness according to your preference.

3. Stir in the green onion, jalapeño, and gochugaru, if desired.

4. Serve with steamed mandu (this sauce is also great over silken tofu).

DALGONA CANDY

5 minutes
Prep time

5 minutes
Cook Time

25 minutes
with cooling time
Total Time

Level: ★★★☆

Makes 1 large or 3 small

INGREDIENTS

2 tablespoons sugar

½ teaspoon baking soda

TOOLS

Baking sheet

Parchment paper or silicone mat

Wooden chopsticks

Food cutters or cookie cutters

1. Line a baking sheet with parchment paper or a silicone mat.

2. Place the sugar in a small nonstick pan over medium-low heat. Stir continuously until the sugar dissolves completely and turns into a liquid, 3 to 5 minutes, pulling the pan off the heat if it looks like the liquid is darkening. Be careful not to let it burn.

3. Remove from the heat and angle the pan to move the sugar to one side of the pan. Immediately stir in the baking soda. Use wooden chopsticks to stir quickly and thoroughly. The color will change to a light golden.

4. Pour the mixture onto the baking sheet. Be cautious as the mixture will be extremely hot.

5. Let sit for 15 to 20 seconds, then press down with any flat metal surface, like a small pot.

6. Immediately use food cutters or cookie cutters to stamp the candy with a cute design.

7. Let cool and harden completely at room temperature, about 10 minutes.

CHINA:
SHRIMP FRIED RICE + CRAB RANGOONS + STRAWBERRY & GRAPE BING TANGHULU

This China-inspired lunch features shrimp fried rice and crab rangoon. Dip the crispy crab rangoon in a sweet chili sauce and finish off with strawberry and grape bing tanghulu, a classic Chinese street food that can be made with a variety of different fruits, for a crunchy, delightful treat. My girls absolutely love it!

SHRIMP FRIED RICE

10 minutes
Prep time

15 minutes
Cook Time

25 minutes
Total Time

Level: ★★☆☆	Serves 2 to 4

1. Heat 2 tablespoons of vegetable oil in a large skillet or wok over medium-high heat.

2. Add the onion and garlic and sauté until fragrant and slightly softened, 2 to 3 minutes.

3. Add the shrimp and cook until they turn pink and are cooked through, 2 to 3 minutes per side. Remove the shrimp from the skillet and set aside.

4. Add the remaining 2 tablespoons of vegetable oil to the skillet. Add the peas and carrots and stir-fry until heated through, about 2 minutes.

5. Add the rice and break it up with a spatula, stirring to combine with the vegetables. Stir in the soy sauce and oyster sauce.

6. Make a well in the middle of the rice and vegetables and pour the eggs in. Lightly scramble the eggs until fully cooked, 2 to 3 minutes.

7. Return the shrimp, onion, and garlic to the skillet and stir-fry until heated through, 2 to 3 more minutes.

8. Season with salt and pepper to taste, then garnish with green onions.

INGREDIENTS

4 tablespoons vegetable oil, divided

½ cup (80 g) diced onion

2 garlic cloves, minced

½ pound (227 g) medium shrimp, peeled and deveined

1 cup (150 g) frozen peas and carrots, thawed

2½ cups (625 g) cooked long-grain rice (preferably day-old)

2 tablespoons soy sauce

1 tablespoon oyster sauce

2 eggs, beaten

Kosher salt and black pepper

Chopped or shredded green onions, for garnish

CRAB RANGOONS

15 minutes
Prep time

10 minutes
Cook Time

25 minutes
Total Time

Level: ★★☆☆	Makes 10

INGREDIENTS

8 ounces (227 g) cream cheese, softened

½ cup (113 g) canned crabmeat or imitation crab, drained and flaked

2 green onions, finely chopped

1 garlic clove, minced

1 teaspoon Worcestershire sauce

Kosher salt and black pepper

10 square wonton wrappers

Vegetable oil

Sweet and sour sauce, for serving, optional

TOOLS
Deep-fry thermometer

1. In a medium bowl, combine the cream cheese, crab, green onions, garlic, Worcestershire sauce, and salt and black pepper to taste. Mix well to combine.

2. Lay out a wonton wrapper on a clean surface. Spoon about 1 tablespoon of the mixture onto the center of the wrapper.

3. Brush the edges of the wrapper with a little water. Lift two opposing corners of the wrapper and pinch only the tip. Then lift the adjacent corners and seal them together. Make sure to pinch them very well to prevent leakage as you fry. Repeat with the remaining wrappers and mixture.

4. Heat enough vegetable oil to submerge the rangoons in a medium pot over medium heat to 350°F (175°C).

5. Carefully place a few rangoons into the hot oil, being careful not to overcrowd the pan. Fry, flipping once halfway through, until golden brown and crispy, 2 to 3 minutes.

6. Use a slotted spoon or tongs to remove the fried rangoons from the oil and transfer them to a paper towel–lined plate to drain.

7. Repeat steps 5 and 6 with the remaining rangoons.

8. Serve hot with sweet and sour sauce, if desired.

AIR FRYER: Spray the air fryer basket with cooking spray to prevent sticking. Place the rangoons in a single layer, making sure they are not touching. Cook in the air fryer at 375°F (190°C) for 6 to 8 minutes, flipping them halfway through, until they are golden brown and crispy.

STRAWBERRY & GRAPE BING TANGHULU

15 minutes	20 minutes	1 hour
Prep time	Cook Time	(with cooling)
		Total Time

Level: ★★☆☆   **Makes 7**

INGREDIENTS

12 to 15 fresh strawberries, washed and stemmed

12 to 15 grapes

2 cups (400 g) sugar

TOOLS

Baking sheet

Parchment paper

Bamboo skewers or lollipop sticks

Candy thermometer

Wooden chopsticks

1. Line a baking sheet with parchment paper. Fill a tall glass with ice water.

2. Thread the strawberries and grapes onto skewers, alternating between the two fruits, leaving some space at the bottom for holding.

3. In a small saucepan, combine the sugar and 1 cup (240 ml) water. Heat over medium heat, gently shaking the pan to move the sugar around until it completely dissolves, 3 to 5 minutes. Do not stir.

4. Simmer for 20 to 25 minutes, until the mixture thickens and the temperature reaches 300°F (150°C). It should be a light amber color. To check if the syrup is ready, dip a wooden chopstick into the syrup, then dip it into the ice water for 10 seconds. It should be crunchy, not sticky. If it is not ready, cook for a couple more minutes to thicken.

5. Carefully tilt the pan so the dissolved sugar is on one side and dip each fruit skewer into the hot syrup, turning to coat evenly. Allow any excess syrup to drip off. Be careful!

6. Place the skewers on the baking sheet to cool and harden for about 30 minutes. To speed up the process, you can submerge each tanghulu into the glass of ice water for 10 to 30 seconds to harden.

7. Let cool and enjoy the same day.

CHINA:

HONEY WALNUT SHRIMP + MANGO PANCAKE POCKETS

This lunch offers a fusion of sweet and savory flavors. Crispy walnuts and tender shrimp lay perfectly on top of a bed of steamed white rice. To balance out the meal, serve with a side of sautéed baby bok choy. For dessert, one of my all-time favorites: Hong Kong–style mango pancake, known as 芒果班戟 (mánggu ǒ bān jǐ) in Chinese. It's a thin, crêpe-like pancake filled with fresh mango slices and whipped cream. It's sweet but not too sweet! Serve with pineapple flowers and raspberries.

"Tom's Diner" — **Suzanne Vega**

"The journey of a thousand miles begins with a single step."
—LAO TZU

HONEY WALNUT SHRIMP

15 minutes
Prep time

10 minutes
Cook Time

25 minutes
Total Time

| Level: ★★☆☆ | | Serves 4 |

1. Line a baking sheet with parchment paper.

2. In a small saucepan, combine the sugar and ¾ cup (180 ml) water. Heat over medium heat until the sugar dissolves completely, 3 to 5 minutes. Let cool.

3. In a nonstick pan, toast the walnuts over medium heat until lightly browned and fragrant, 5 minutes. Remove from the heat. Mix with the sugar syrup, and spread out on the baking sheet to cool.

4. In a large bowl, whisk together the mayonnaise, honey, condensed milk, lemon juice, and salt. Set aside.

5. Heat 1 to 2 inches (3 to 5 cm) of vegetable oil in a large skillet to 350°F (175°C).

6. Place the cornstarch in a shallow bowl, then add the shrimp and toss to evenly coat, shaking off any excess. Carefully lower the shrimp into the hot oil and fry until golden brown and crispy, 3 to 4 minutes, working in batches. Transfer to paper towels to drain.

7. Add the shrimp to the sauce and toss to coat. Add the walnuts and gently mix them in.

8. Serve warm over rice, top with green onions, and enjoy!

INGREDIENTS

½ cup (100 g) sugar

1 cup (100 g) walnuts

¼ cup (60 ml) mayonnaise

2 tablespoons honey

1 tablespoon condensed milk

1 tablespoon lemon juice

½ teaspoon kosher salt

Vegetable oil

⅓ cup (40 g) cornstarch

1 pound (454 g) large shrimp, peeled and deveined

Cooked white rice, for serving

Sliced green onions, for garnish

TOOLS

Parchment paper

Baking sheet

MANGO PANCAKE POCKETS

15 minutes
Prep time

10 minutes
Cook Time

25 minutes
Total Time

Level: ★★☆☆

Makes 6 to 8

1. Make the pancakes: In a large bowl, combine the eggs, milk, flour, sugar, cornstarch, vanilla, and salt. Whisk until smooth.

2. Heat a nonstick frying pan over medium heat. Add in 1 to 2 tablespoons of vegetable oil to coat the pan. Pour a ladleful of the batter onto the pan and swirl it around to create a thin, round pancake. Cook until lightly golden, 1 to 2 minutes on each side. Repeat with the remaining batter.

3. Make the filling: To a medium bowl, add the cream and sugar. Use a hand mixer to whip until it thickens and forms soft peaks, 2 to 3 minutes.

4. Assemble the pancake pockets: Place a pancake on a plate and spread 2 tablespoons of whipped cream in the center. Arrange a mango slice on top of the cream.

5. Roll up the pancake tightly, starting from the bottom to the middle, then the sides, and closing the top down, enclosing the filling like a burrito.

6. Repeat steps 5 and 6 with the remaining pancakes, whipped cream, and mango slices.

7. Cut crosswise. Serve right away or chill in the fridge until ready to eat!

INGREDIENTS

4 eggs

¾ cup (200 ml) milk

1 cup (120 g) all-purpose flour

2 tablespoons sugar

1 tablespoon cornstarch

1 teaspoon vanilla extract

¼ teaspoon kosher salt

Vegetable oil

FILLING

⅔ cup (150 ml) heavy whipping cream

1 tablespoon sugar

2 ripe mangos, peeled and cut into 1 x 2-inch (2.5 x 5 cm) pieces

TOOLS

Hand or stand mixer

"Cough Syrup" — **Young the Giant**

The harder you work for something, the greater you'll feel when you achieve it.

MEXICO:

COCTEL DE CAMARONES + MEXICAN RICE + HORCHATA

My two eldest girls are proud of their Mexican heritage, and I enjoy incorporating it into their lunches. Join us in celebrating Mexican culture through this delicious meal, which includes coctel de camarones, flower-shaped tortilla chips, Mexican rice, and sweet horchata to drink. Embrace the flavors of Mexico as you savor each bite.

COCTEL DE CAMARONES
(SHRIMP COCKTAIL)

20 minutes
Prep time

10 minutes
Cook Time

1 hour
with chill time
Total Time

Level: ★☆☆☆

Serves 4

INGREDIENTS

1 pound (454 g) large shrimp, peeled and deveined, tails removed

2 cups (240 ml) clamato juice

¼ cup (60 ml) ketchup

2 tablespoons lime juice

1 tablespoon hot sauce, such as Cholula or Tapatio

1 cucumber, diced

3 roma tomatoes, diced

½ red onion, diced

¼ cup (10 g) chopped cilantro

Kosher salt and black pepper

1 avocado, diced

Tortilla chips or saltine crackers, for serving

1. Fill a large pot halfway with water and bring to a boil. Add the shrimp and cook until pink and cooked through, 2 to 3 minutes. Drain in a colander, run under cool water, and let cool.

2. In a large bowl, mix the clamato juice, ketchup, lime juice, and hot sauce.

3. Add the shrimp, cucumber, tomatoes, onion, and cilantro. Gently toss to coat.

4. Season with salt and pepper to taste and stir again. Gently fold in the diced avocado.

5. Cover the bowl and refrigerate for 30 minutes to 1 hour to allow the flavors to meld.

6. Serve chilled with a side of tortilla chips or crackers. Perfect for lunches the following day!

MEXICAN RICE

10 minutes
Prep time

30 minutes
Cook Time

45 minutes
with rest time
Total Time

Level: ★☆☆☆

Serves 4

INGREDIENTS

1 cup (200 g) long-grain white rice

2 tablespoons vegetable oil, plus more as needed

½ yellow onion, diced

1 bell pepper (any color), diced

2 garlic cloves, minced

One 8-ounce (227 g) can tomato sauce

1¾ cups (420 ml) chicken or vegetable broth

1 teaspoon chicken bouillon

1 teaspoon ground cumin

1 teaspoon chili powder

Kosher salt and black pepper

Chopped fresh cilantro

1. Rinse the rice under cold water until the water runs clear. Shake the strainer to remove as much water as possible and let drain.

2. Heat the oil in a large skillet, pot, or Dutch oven over medium heat. Add the rice and cook, stirring frequently, until dried and golden brown, 5 to 9 minutes, stirring often and scraping the bottom of the pan.

3. If your pan is dry, add a splash of oil. Add the onion, pepper, and garlic and cook until softened, 2 to 3 minutes.

4. Stir in the tomato sauce, broth, chicken bouillon, cumin, and chili powder. Add salt and black pepper to taste.

5. Bring to a boil, then reduce the heat to low and cover. Cook for about 20 minutes, until the rice is cooked through and the liquid is absorbed.

6. Remove from the heat and let sit, covered, for an additional 5 minutes to steam.

7. Fluff the rice with a rice scooper or fork, taste for additional salt and pepper, and sprinkle with freshly chopped cilantro before serving.

HORCHATA

5 minutes
Prep time

0 minutes
Cook Time

5 hours
with chill time
Total Time

Level: ★☆☆☆

Makes about 6 cups (1.4 L)

INGREDIENTS

1 cup (200 g) long-grain white rice

2 cinnamon sticks

½ cup (100 g) sugar

2 teaspoons vanilla extract

1 cup (240 ml) whole milk (optional)

Ground cinnamon

Ice cubes

TOOLS

Fine mesh strainer or cheesecloth

1. Rinse the rice under cold water until the water runs clear.

2. In a blender, combine the rice, cinnamon sticks, and 4 cups (960 ml) water. Blend on high, in batches if necessary, until the mixture is well combined and the rice starts to break down, 1 to 2 minutes.

3. Pour the mixture into a container with a lid and let it sit in the fridge for at least 4 hours or overnight, to allow the flavors to infuse and the rice to soften.

4. Pour the rice mixture into the blender and blend for 1 to 2 minutes, until smooth and creamy.

5. Place a fine-mesh strainer or cheesecloth over a large bowl or pitcher. Pour the mixture through the strainer, using a spoon to press out as much liquid as possible. Discard any remaining solids.

6. Stir in the sugar and vanilla until well combined. If desired, stir in milk for a creamier texture.

7. Cover and refrigerate for at least 1 hour to chill.

8. Serve over ice. Sprinkle cinnamon on top for extra flavor and decoration.

MEXICO:
POZOLE + HOMEMADE TORTILLAS + ROASTED RED SALSA

This Mexican lunch features pozole, a flavorful and hearty soup made with hominy and pork, served with homemade tortillas. Homemade tortillas are the best! Serve with roasted red salsa for a touch of smoky heat, fresh limes, and radishes on the side to add brightness and crunch.

POZOLE

15 minutes	**2 ½ hours**	**2 hours and 45 minutes**
Prep time	Cook Time	Total Time

Level: ★★☆☆ **Serves 2 to 4**

1. In a large pot, combine the pork, onion, garlic, broth, chicken bouillon, oregano, and cumin. Season with salt and pepper to taste.

2. Bring to a boil over medium-high heat, then reduce the heat to low and simmer for 60 to 90 minutes, until the pork is tender.

3. Meanwhile, soak the ancho and guajillo chiles in hot water for 10 minutes. Drain and rinse the chiles. In a blender or food processor, blend the chiles with 3 to 4 tablespoons of water to create a smooth paste.

4. Remove the pork with a slotted spoon, shred with two forks, and return to the pot.

5. Add the chile paste and hominy. Stir well.

6. Simmer for 20 to 30 minutes to allow the flavors to meld. Taste and adjust the salt and pepper.

7. Serve the pozole hot, topped with shredded cabbage, radishes, chopped cilantro, avocado, and lime wedges, with warm tortillas on the side.

INGREDIENTS

1 pound (454 g) boneless pork shoulder, trimmed and cut into 1-inch (2.5 cm) chunks

1 onion, diced

3 garlic cloves, smashed

4 cups (960 ml) chicken broth

1 teaspoon chicken bouillon

1 teaspoon dried oregano

1 teaspoon ground cumin

Kosher salt and black pepper

2 dried ancho chiles, seeded

2 dried guajillo chiles, seeded

Two 15-ounce (425 g) cans hominy, drained and rinsed

Homemade Tortillas (page 204), for serving

TOPPINGS (OPTIONAL)

Shredded cabbage

Sliced radishes

Chopped cilantro

Sliced avocado

Lime wedges

HOMEMADE TORTILLAS

10 minutes	10 minutes	20 minutes
Prep time	Cook Time	Total Time

Level: ★★☆☆   **Makes 8 to 10**

1. In a large bowl, whisk together the flour and salt.

2. Use your fingers to work the butter into the flour mixture until the butter is pea-sized.

3. Gradually stir in ½ cup (120 ml) warm water with a spoon or mix with your hands until a dough starts to form. Add more water, 1 teaspoon at a time, until the dough comes together, and is well hydrated, but not sticky.

4. Turn the dough out onto a lightly floured surface and knead until smooth and elastic, about 5 minutes. If the dough feels sticky, add a little more flour.

5. Divide the dough into eight to ten golf ball–sized portions. Cover with a kitchen towel and let rest for 10 to 15 minutes.

6. Take a dough ball and, adding more flour as needed, flatten it using your hands or a rolling pin into a ⅛-inch-thick (3 mm) circle. Repeat with the remaining dough.

7. Heat a medium skillet or nonstick pan over medium-high heat. Brush lightly with oil.

8. Place one dough round in the skillet and cook until it bubbles and puffs up slightly, about 30 seconds.

9. Flip the tortilla and cook for another 30 seconds, until golden-brown spots appear.

10. Remove the tortilla from the skillet and wrap in a kitchen towel to keep it warm and pliable.

11. Repeat the cooking process with the remaining dough, adding a little more oil to the skillet as needed. Serve warm.

TO STORE: Homemade tortillas will keep for up to 3 days. Let them cool completely, then place them in an airtight container or resealable bag with parchment or wax paper between them to prevent sticking. Seal the container tightly, then store in the refrigerator. To serve, warm the tortillas in a skillet or microwave for a few seconds to make them soft and pliable.

INGREDIENTS

2 cups (240 g) all-purpose flour, plus more for dusting

¼ teaspoon kosher salt

4 tablespoons softened butter, cubed

Vegetable oil

TOOLS

Rolling pin

ROASTED RED SALSA

5 minutes
Prep time

10 minutes
Cook Time

15 minutes
Total Time

Level: ★☆☆☆

Makes 2½ cups (600 ml)

1. In a dry skillet over medium heat, toast the chiles until fragrant, 1 to 2 minutes. Be careful not to burn them.
2. Preheat your broiler on high. Line a rimmed baking sheet with aluminum foil.
3. Place the tomatoes cut side down on the baking sheet. Add the garlic cloves.
4. Broil for 5 to 7 minutes, until the tomato skins are charred and blistered.
5. Transfer the tomatoes to a blender or food processor. Add the chiles, garlic, and salt. Blend until smooth.
6. Taste and adjust the salt if needed. Serve with tortilla chips.

×

INGREDIENTS

6 dried árbol chiles

5 to 6 ripe Roma or plum tomatoes, cored and halved

4 garlic cloves, peeled

1 teaspoon kosher salt

Tortilla chips, for serving

TOOLS

Baking sheet

Aluminium foil

Blender

"The only way to achieve the impossible is to believe it is possible."

—CHARLES KINGSLEIGH, ALICE IN WONDERLAND

"Linger" — **The Cranberries**

INDIA:

PANEER TIKKA MASALA + TURMERIC RICE

This paneer tikka masala is my little sister's favorite. Succulent paneer cheese is marinated in a medley of spices, cooked to perfection, and simmered in a rich, tomato-based sauce. Serve alongside fragrant turmeric rice. I added starfruit, crispy kale chips, and toasted corn nuts that provide a satisfying texture to complete this culinary journey.

PANEER TIKKA MASALA

10 minutes	40 minutes	3 hours
Prep time	Cook Time	with marinating
		Total Time

Level: ★★★☆   **Serves 4**

1. In a large bowl, combine the yogurt, ginger-garlic paste, lemon juice, oil, coriander, cumin, garam masala, turmeric, and salt.

2. Add the paneer and toss gently to coat. Let marinate for at least 30 minutes or up to 2 hours for better flavor.

3. Preheat your oven to 400°F (200°C). Line a baking sheet with parchment paper.

4. Place the paneer on the baking sheet.

5. Bake for 15 to 20 minutes, until lightly browned and slightly crispy. Flip halfway through cooking for even browning.

6. Make the sauce: In a large pan, heat the oil over medium heat. Add the onion and sauté until golden brown, 5 to 7 minutes.

7. Add the ginger-garlic paste and sauté until golden, 30 seconds to 1 minute.

8. Stir in the tomato puree and tomato paste and cook until the oil starts to separate from the mixture, 3 to 4 minutes.

9. Add the red chili powder, garam masala, coriander, cumin, turmeric, and salt to taste. Mix well and cook for another 2 minutes.

10. Reduce the heat to low and stir in the heavy cream. Blend the sauce with an immersion blender until smooth.

11. Add the paneer cubes and gently mix them, ensuring each piece is coated with the sauce. Simmer for 5 minutes to let the flavors meld.

12. Garnish with fresh cilantro leaves and serve.

INGREDIENTS

½ cup (120 ml) plain Greek yogurt

1 tablespoon ginger-garlic paste

1 tablespoon fresh lemon juice

1 tablespoon vegetable oil

1 teaspoon ground coriander

1 teaspoon ground cumin

1 teaspoon garam masala

1 teaspoon ground turmeric

1 teaspoon kosher salt

8 ounces (227 g) paneer, cubed

Fresh cilantro leaves

MASALA SAUCE

2 tablespoons vegetable oil

1 large onion, finely chopped

1 tablespoon ginger-garlic paste

One 10¾-ounce (305 g) can tomato puree

1 tablespoon tomato paste

2 teaspoons red chili powder

1½ teaspoons garam masala

1 teaspoon ground coriander

1 teaspoon ground cumin

1 teaspoon ground turmeric

Kosher salt

¼ cup (60 ml) heavy cream

TOOLS

Baking sheet

Parchment paper

Immersion blender

TURMERIC RICE

5 minutes
Prep time

25 minutes
Cook Time

30 minutes
Total Time

Level: ★☆☆☆

Serves 2

1. Rinse the rice under cold water until the water runs clear.

2. In a medium pot, heat the butter over medium heat.

3. Add the onion and sauté until translucent and lightly golden brown, 3 to 5 minutes. Stir in the garlic. Cook until fragrant, 1 minute.

4. Add the rice and toast for a few minutes, stirring occasionally.

5. In a small bowl, dissolve the turmeric in 2 teaspoons of water to form a paste. Add the paste to the pot and mix well, ensuring all the rice is evenly coated.

6. Pour in 2 cups (480 ml) water and season with salt to taste. Increase the heat to high and bring the mixture to a boil, then reduce the heat to low and cover with a tight-fitting lid. Simmer for 15 to 20 minutes, until all the water is absorbed and the rice is cooked through.

7. Remove the pot from the heat and let sit, covered, for 5 minutes to allow the steam to finish cooking the rice and fluff it up.

8. Before serving, gently fluff the rice with a rice scooper. Garnish with fresh cilantro leaves.

INGREDIENTS

1 cup (200 g) white basmati rice

1 tablespoon butter

½ cup (80 g) finely chopped onion

2 garlic cloves, minced

1 teaspoon ground turmeric

Kosher salt

Fresh cilantro leaves

BUTTER CHICKEN + GARLIC NAAN + MANGO CHUTNEY

Experience the rich flavors of India with this creamy butter chicken paired with fluffy garlic naan, zesty mango chutney, and crispy popped chickpeas. Serve the butter chicken with rice or dip the garlic naan into the delicious sauce.

BUTTER CHICKEN

10 minutes	**35 minutes**	**45 minutes**
Prep time	Cook Time	Total Time

Level: ★★☆☆ **Serves 4**

1. Heat the ghee in a large pan over medium heat. Add the onion and sauté until golden brown, 5 to 7 minutes.

2. Add the garlic and ginger and cook until golden, 1 more minute.

3. In a small bowl, mix the coriander, cumin, red chili powder, and turmeric. Add the mixture to the pan and cook for a minute to release the flavors.

4. Add the chicken and cook until no longer pink on the outside, 10 to 12 minutes.

5. Stir in the tomato puree and cook until the sauce thickens slightly, 5 to 7 minutes.

6. Reduce the heat to low and stir in the yogurt. Simmer for about 10 minutes, allowing the flavors to meld. Stir in the heavy cream and continue to simmer for another 5 minutes.

7. Add the butter and season with salt to taste. Stir until the butter is melted and well combined.

8. Drizzle with yogurt, garnish with cilantro, and serve hot with steamed rice or garlic naan.

INGREDIENTS

2 tablespoons ghee or vegetable oil

1 large onion, finely chopped

2 garlic cloves, minced

One 1-inch (2.5 cm) piece of ginger, grated

2 teaspoons ground coriander

2 teaspoons ground cumin

1 teaspoon red chili powder

1 teaspoon ground turmeric

1 pound (454 g) boneless chicken thighs or breast, cut into bite-size pieces

1 cup (240 ml) tomato puree

½ cup (120 ml) plain yogurt, plus more for serving

½ cup (120 ml) heavy cream or half-and-half

2 tablespoons butter

Kosher salt

Fresh cilantro leaves

FOR SERVING

Steamed rice

Garlic Naan (page 212)

GARLIC NAAN

15 minutes
Prep time

15 minutes
Cook Time

2 ½ hours
with rest time
Total Time

Level: ★★☆☆

Makes 8

1. In a large bowl, combine the flour, yeast, sugar, and salt. Add the yogurt and butter and mix well.

2. Gradually add ¾ cup (180 ml) warm water, a little at a time (you may not need all of it), kneading the dough until it comes together. Adjust the amount of water to form a soft and smooth dough.

3. Transfer the dough to a lightly floured surface and knead until elastic, about 5 minutes.

4. Place the dough in a butter-greased bowl, cover it with a damp cloth, and let it rest in a warm place for 1 to 2 hours until it doubles in size.

5. Punch the dough down to release any air bubbles. Knead again for a few minutes.

6. Divide the dough into eight to ten small, equal-sized balls.

7. Take one dough ball at a time and roll it out into an oval or circle, about ¼-inch (6 mm) thick.

8. Sprinkle the garlic on top and gently press it into the dough.

9. Heat a skillet over medium-high heat. Brush lightly with ghee or vegetable oil.

10. Place one naan, garlic side up, onto the hot skillet and cook until bubbles start to form on the surface, 1 to 2 minutes. Flip and cook until nicely toasted, 1 more minute.

11. Remove the naan from the skillet and brush it with butter. Sprinkle on some chopped cilantro, if desired.

12. Repeat steps 10 and 11 with the remaining dough.

13. Serve hot with mango chutney or your favorite Indian dish.

INGREDIENTS

x

2 cups (250 g) all-purpose flour, plus more for dusting

1 teaspoon instant yeast

1 teaspoon sugar

½ teaspoon kosher salt

¼ cup (60 ml) plain yogurt

2 tablespoons melted butter or vegetable oil, plus more for greasing

4 garlic cloves, minced

Ghee or vegetable oil, for brushing

Chopped fresh cilantro leaves, optional

Mango Chutney (page 213), for serving

MANGO CHUTNEY

10 minutes	40 minutes	50 minutes
Prep time	Cook Time	Total Time

Level: ★☆☆☆ | **Makes 3 cups (750 g)**

1. In a medium saucepan, combine the mangoes, onion, sugar, vinegar, garlic, ginger, mustard seeds, red pepper flakes, turmeric, and salt to taste. Bring to a boil over medium heat.

2. Reduce the heat to low and simmer for 30 to 40 minutes, stirring occasionally, until the mangoes are soft and the chutney has thickened to your desired consistency.

3. Taste and add more sugar or red pepper flakes if needed.

4. Remove from the heat and let cool completely.

5. This will keep for up to 2 weeks in sterilized jars in the refrigerator.

HOW TO STERILIZE JARS:

1. Clean the jars: Wash the jars and lids in hot soapy water, then rinse them thoroughly.

2. Fill a large pot with enough water to fully submerge the jars. Place the clean jars and lids into the pot, making sure they are completely submerged.

3. Bring the water to a rolling boil and let the jars boil for 10 minutes.

4. Using jar tongs or heat-resistant gloves, carefully remove the hot jars from the boiling water, allowing any excess water to drain off.

5. Let the jars cool at room temperature and air dry.

INGREDIENTS

2 large ripe mangoes, peeled, pitted, and diced

1 small onion, finely chopped

1 cup (200 g) sugar

½ cup (120 ml) white vinegar

2 garlic cloves, minced

1 teaspoon grated ginger

1 teaspoon mustard seeds

½ teaspoon red pepper flakes

½ teaspoon ground turmeric

Kosher salt

TOOLS

Sterilized jars

"It Ain't Over 'til It's Over" — **Lenny Kravitz**

THAILAND:

TOFU PAD SEE EW + GARLIC GREEN BEANS + MANGO STICKY RICE

This lunch will bring you on a culinary journey to Thailand. Tofu pad see ew, a classic Thai dish, is made with chewy rice noodles, tofu, and a savory soy sauce. This was one of the first Thai dishes I tried cooking at home! Garlic green beans, lightly sautéed with fragrant garlic, are a delightful side that perfectly complements the main dish. For a sweet ending to your meal, enjoy mango sticky rice, a Thai dessert featuring ripe mango slices and sticky, coconut milk–infused rice.

You're crushing it! Keep up the great work!

TOFU PAD SEE EW

15 minutes	25 minutes	40 minutes
Prep time	Cook Time	Total Time

Level: ★★☆☆   **Serves 4**

1. Cook the noodles, according to package directions, until al dente. Drain and set aside.

2. In a small bowl, combine the oyster sauce, soy sauce, dark soy sauce, and brown sugar.

3. Heat the vegetable oil in a large pan or wok over medium-high heat. Add the tofu and cook until golden brown on all sides, 10 to 15 minutes. Remove from the pan and set aside.

4. To the same pan, add a little more oil if needed, then add the garlic and sauté until fragrant, 1 minute.

5. Add the bok choy and stir-fry until they start to soften, 5 to 7 minutes.

6. Push the vegetables to one side of the pan and pour the eggs into the empty space. Scramble the eggs until cooked through, 2 to 3 minutes.

7. Add the noodles, tofu, and sauce mixture. Toss everything together until the noodles are well coated with the sauce and heated through. Taste and season with salt and pepper if needed.

8. Remove from the heat and serve hot. Garnish with lime wedges and cilantro, if desired.

INGREDIENTS

½ pound (227 g) flat rice noodles

2 tablespoons oyster sauce or vegetarian substitute

2 tablespoons soy sauce

1 tablespoon dark soy sauce

1 tablespoon brown sugar

2 tablespoons vegetable oil, plus more as needed

12 ounces (340 g) firm tofu, drained and cubed

2 garlic cloves, minced

3 cups (255 g) baby bok choy, halved

2 eggs, beaten, optional

Kosher salt and black pepper

FOR SERVING (OPTIONAL)

Lime wedges

Chopped cilantro

GARLIC GREEN BEANS

10 minutes
Prep time

10 minutes
Cook Time

20 minutes
Total Time

Level: ★☆☆☆

Serves 4

INGREDIENTS

2 tablespoons vegetable oil

3 garlic cloves, minced

1 pound (454 g) green beans, trimmed

2 tablespoons soy sauce

1 tablespoon oyster sauce

1 teaspoon sugar

½ teaspoon red pepper flakes, optional

Kosher salt

1. Heat the vegetable oil in a large pan or wok over medium-high heat. Add the garlic and sauté until fragrant, about 1 minute.

2. Add the green beans and stir-fry until bright green and slightly tender, about 5 minutes.

3. In a small bowl, whisk together the soy sauce, oyster sauce, sugar, and red pepper flakes, if using.

4. Pour the sauce mixture over the green beans and toss to coat evenly. Cook, stirring frequently, until the green beans have reached your desired level of tenderness, another 2 to 3 minutes. Taste and season with salt if needed.

5. Remove from the heat and serve as a side dish with rice or noodles.

MANGO STICKY RICE

4 hours
Prep time

25 minutes
Cook Time

4 hours and 25 minutes
Total Time

Level: ★★☆☆

Serves 4

INGREDIENTS

1 cup (200 g) glutinous rice

1 cup (240 ml) coconut milk

½ cup (100 g) sugar

¼ teaspoon kosher salt

2 ripe mangoes, peeled and sliced

Sesame seeds, optional

TOOLS

Cheesecloth or banana leaf

Steamer

1. Rinse the rice with cold water until the water runs clear. Soak the rice in water for at least 4 hours or overnight.

2. Drain the rice and transfer it to a steamer lined with cheesecloth or a banana leaf. Steam the rice over medium heat until tender and cooked through, 20 to 25 minutes.

3. Meanwhile, prepare the coconut sauce: Combine the coconut milk, sugar, and salt in a small saucepan. Heat over low heat, stirring occasionally, until the sugar has dissolved. Do not let it boil.

4. Transfer the rice to a bowl and pour in half of the coconut sauce. Stir gently to coat the rice evenly.

5. To serve, place a portion of the sticky rice on a plate or in a bowl. Top it with a few mango slices. Drizzle on more coconut sauce and sprinkle some sesame seeds on top for added texture and flavor, if desired.

TIP: Mold the sticky rice into a heart shape when adding to a lunch!

PHILIPPINES:
CHICKEN ADOBO + GARLIC FRIED RICE + GINATAANG BILO BILO

My stepmom is Filipina, and I have always cherished the flavors of her cooking, especially her beloved chicken adobo. This garlic fried rice is a favorite any time of day, and the comforting sweetness of ginataang bilo bilo (rice balls in coconut milk) is a satisfying end to the meal.

GARLIC FRIED RICE

5 minutes
Prep time

15 minutes
Cook Time

20 minutes
Total Time

| Level: ★☆☆☆ | Makes 4 cups (800 g) |

INGREDIENTS

2 tablespoons vegetable oil

6 garlic cloves, minced

4 cups (800 g) cooked jasmine rice (preferably day-old)

1 tablespoon soy sauce, optional

Kosher salt and black pepper

Sliced green onions, optional

1. Heat the vegetable oil in a large skillet or wok over medium heat.

2. Add the garlic and sauté until fragrant and golden brown, 1 to 2 minutes. Be careful not to burn the garlic.

3. Add the rice and stir-fry for 5 to 7 minutes, ensuring that the rice is evenly coated with the oil and garlic.

4. If desired, add the soy sauce. Stir-fry for another 1 to 2 minutes. Season with salt and pepper to taste.

5. Continue stir-frying until the rice is heated through and has a slightly crispy texture, 5 to 7 minutes.

6. Transfer to a serving dish and garnish with sliced green onions, if desired.

CHICKEN ADOBO

40 minutes
(with marinating time)
Prep time

1 hour
Cook Time

1 hour 40 minutes
Total Time

Level: ★★☆☆

Serves 4

1. In a large bowl, combine the soy sauce and soda. Add the chicken and marinate for at least 30 minutes in the refrigerator.

2. Heat the oil in a large skillet or pot over medium heat. Remove the chicken from the marinade, reserving the marinade, and brown the chicken pieces on all sides, 6 to 8 minutes. Remove the chicken from the skillet and set aside.

3. In the same skillet, sauté the onion, garlic, and ginger until fragrant and slightly translucent, 3 to 5 minutes.

4. Add the potatoes and cook, 3 to 5 minutes.

5. Return the chicken to the skillet. Pour in the reserved marinade, along with the bay leaves, black peppercorns, and brown sugar, if using. Stir together.

6. Bring to a boil, then reduce the heat to low and cover the skillet. Let it simmer for 20 to 25 minutes, until the chicken is cooked through.

7. Flip the chicken over and add the vinegar. Cover and continue simmering for another 20 to 25 minutes, until the chicken is tender and the potatoes are tender and cooked through.

8. Taste the sauce and adjust the salt if needed.

9. Serve hot with rice.

INGREDIENTS

½ cup (120 ml) soy sauce

¼ cup (60 ml) lemon-lime soda, such as Sprite

1 tablespoon vegetable oil

2 pounds (1 kg) bone-in chicken pieces

½ yellow onion, roughly chopped

3 garlic cloves, minced

1½ teaspoons minced ginger

2 medium Yukon Gold potatoes, peeled and quartered

2 bay leaves

½ teaspoon whole black peppercorns

1½ teaspoons brown sugar, optional

⅓ cup (80 ml) white vinegar, plus more more to taste

Kosher salt

Garlic Fried Rice (page 219) or steamed rice, for serving

GINATAANG BILO BILO

(RICE BALLS IN COCONUT MILK)

10 minutes	40 minutes	50 minutes
Prep time	Cook Time	Total Time

Level: ★★★☆	Serves 4

INGREDIENTS

1 cup (160 g) glutinous rice flour

1 medium sweet potato, peeled and cubed

One 13.5-ounce (398 ml) can coconut milk

Pandan leaves, optional

1 cup (200 g) sago pearls (tapioca pearls), fresh or canned

1 cup (200 g) sliced ripe jackfruit

3 tablespoons sugar

1. In a small bowl, combine the glutinous rice flour and slowly add ½ cup (120 ml) water, while mixing with your hands to form a smooth dough. Take 1½ teaspoons of dough at a time and roll into a small ball. Set aside.

2. Place the sweet potato cubes in a large pot and fill with enough water to cover them. Bring to a boil and cook until tender, 20 minutes. Drain and set aside.

3. To the same pot, add the coconut milk, 1 cup (240 ml) water, and pandan leaves, if using. Bring to a simmer over medium heat for 15 minutes to blend the flavors.

4. Add the sago pearls and cook until translucent, 10 to 12 minutes. Stir occasionally to prevent sticking.

5. Add the rice balls and cook until they float to the surface and are cooked through but still slightly chewy, 5 to 7 minutes.

6. Add the sweet potato and jackfruit. Stir gently to combine.

7. Add the sugar and stir to dissolve. Simmer for another 5 minutes to allow the flavors to meld.

8. Remove from the heat and let cool slightly before serving. Serve warm or chilled.

◀◀ ▶❚❚ ▶▶

"The Light" — **Common**

"Heroes come and go,
but legends are
forever."
—KOBE BRYANT

PHILIPPINES:
BITE-SIZE PORK LUMPIA + VEGGIE PANCIT + SWEET CHILI DIPPING SAUCE

This lovely Filipino lunch combines veggie pancit, bite-size pork lumpia, and sweet chili dipping sauce, with dried mango slices and rambutan on the side. The pancit features rice noodles stir-fried with colorful vegetables, creating a blend of textures and flavors. The lumpia is crispy on the outside, with a juicy pork filling on the inside. Dip each bite into the tangy dipping sauce for an extra burst of flavor.

BITE-SIZE PORK LUMPIA

30 minutes
Prep time

20 minutes
Cook Time

50 minutes
Total Time

| Level: ★★★☆ | Makes 20 to 25 |

INGREDIENTS

1 pound (454 g) ground pork

1 cup (110 g) grated carrots

1 cup (70 g) shredded cabbage

½ cup (25 g) chopped green onions

3 garlic cloves, minced

1 tablespoon soy sauce

1 tablespoon oyster sauce

1 teaspoon kosher salt

½ teaspoon black pepper

One 12-ounce (340 g) package lumpia or spring roll wrappers

Vegetable oil

Sweet Chili Dipping Sauce (page 225), for serving

1. In a large bowl, combine the pork, carrots, cabbage, green onions, garlic, soy sauce, oyster sauce, salt, and pepper.

2. Using one lumpia wrapper at a time and keeping the rest covered with a dish towel, lay the wrapper on a flat surface. Spoon about 3 tablespoons of the pork mixture onto the center of the wrapper and form a log, leaving a 1-inch (2.5 cm) space on either side.

3. Fold the bottom of the wrapper over the filling and roll it tightly towards the top. Fold the sides of the wrapper in toward the middle and roll almost all the way up. Dab some water at the top edge to seal the lumpia, then set aside and cover with a kitchen towel.

4. Repeat steps 2 and 3 with the remaining wrappers and filling.

5. Using a serrated knife with a sawing motion, cut each lumpia into 2-inch-long (5 cm) pieces.

6. Heat about 1 inch (2.5 cm) of oil in a deep pan or skillet to 350°F (175°C). Fry the lumpia in batches until golden brown and crispy, about 3 minutes per side, returning the oil to temperature between batches. Place them on a paper towel–lined plate to drain.

7. Serve hot with sweet chili sauce for dipping.

AIR FRYER: Lay the lumpias on the air fryer tray. Lightly brush with vegetable oil. Air fry for 8 minutes at 390°F (200°C), then flip and cook for another 6 to 8 minutes, until crispy.

VEGGIE PANCIT

15 minutes
Prep time

15 minutes
Cook Time

30 minutes
Total Time

Level: ★★☆☆

Serves 6

INGREDIENTS

8 ounces (227 g) pancit or rice vermicelli noodles

2 tablespoons vegetable oil

1 small onion, sliced

3 garlic cloves, minced

6 ounces (170 g) green beans, cut into 2-inch (5 cm) pieces

2 medium carrots, julienned

1 green bell pepper, sliced

1 cup (70 g) shredded cabbage

1⅓ cups (100 g) bean sprouts

1 heaping cup (100 g) snow peas

2 tablespoons soy sauce

2 tablespoons oyster sauce

Kosher salt and black pepper

FOR SERVING

Chopped green onions

Chopped cilantro

Calamansi or lemon wedges

1. Cook the noodles according to package directions. Drain, rinse under cool water, and set aside.

2. In a large wok or skillet, heat the oil over medium heat. Add the onion and garlic and cook until fragrant and slightly softened, 2 to 3 minutes.

3. Add the green beans, carrots, bell pepper, and cabbage. Stir-fry until tender-crisp, 3 to 4 minutes. Add the bean sprouts and snow peas and cook until tender, another 2 minutes.

4. Push the vegetables to one side of the pan and add the noodles to the other side. Add the soy sauce and oyster sauce, and toss to combine. Season with salt and black pepper to taste and cook until heated through, 2 to 3 minutes.

5. Remove from the heat and transfer to a serving dish. Garnish with chopped green onions and cilantro.

6. Serve hot with calamansi or lemon wedges on the side.

SWEET CHILI DIPPING SAUCE

5 minutes
Prep time

20 minutes
Cook Time

25 minutes
Total Time

Level: ★☆☆☆

Makes 1⅓ cups (320 ml)

INGREDIENTS

¾ cup (150 g) sugar

½ cup (120 ml) rice vinegar

3 garlic cloves, minced

1 tablespoon red pepper flakes, or to taste

1 tablespoon cornstarch (optional)

1. In a small saucepan, combine the sugar, vinegar, garlic, red pepper flakes, and ½ cup (120 ml) water. Bring to a boil over medium heat, stirring occasionally to dissolve the sugar, 3 to 4 minutes.

2. Reduce the heat and simmer for 10 to 15 minutes, allowing the flavors to meld.

3. For a thicker sauce, make a cornstarch slurry by combining the cornstarch and 2 tablespoons of water in a small bowl. Slowly pour the slurry into the sauce, stirring continuously. Cook for an additional 2 to 3 minutes, until the sauce thickens to your desired consistency.

4. Remove from the heat and let cool before serving.

5. Serve alongside pork lumpia. Store in the fridge for up to 1 week in an airtight container.

"Be kind, have courage,
and always believe in a
little magic."
—CINDERELLA

JAPAN:
YAKI TUNA ONIGIRI + SUNOMONO + GARLIC SOY EDAMAME

Embark on a culinary journey to Japan with this yummy lunch spread. Yaki tuna onigiri, grilled rice balls filled with tuna, offer a delightful contrast of crispy and tender elements that will leave you completely satisfied. Serve with a refreshing cucumber salad, tossed in a zesty dressing. The edamame is coated with a garlic-infused soy sauce that elevates the soybeans to a whole new level of yum. Peach gummies, chocolate covered boba, and a taiyaki wafer add sweet touches to the meal.

YAKI TUNA ONIGIRI

20 minutes
Prep time

20 minutes
Cook Time

40 minutes
Total Time

Level: ★★☆☆	Makes 8

INGREDIENTS

One 5-ounce (142 g) can tuna in water, drained

1 tablespoon soy sauce

1½ teaspoons Japanese mayonnaise, such as Kewpie

1½ teaspoons mirin (Japanese sweet rice wine)

1½ teaspoons sesame oil

2 teaspoons sugar

Vegetable oil

2 cups (200 g) cooked and cooled sushi rice

Nori sheets, cut into 1-inch (2.5 cm) strips

TOOLS

Onigiri mold

1. In a medium bowl, combine the tuna, soy sauce, mayonnaise, mirin, sesame oil, and sugar. Mix well.

2. Brush a little vegetable oil inside the onigiri mold to prevent the rice from sticking (you can skip this step if using a nonstick mold).

3. Add 2 tablespoons of rice to the mold, pressing down with a small spoon dipped in water to make it compact.

4. Fill the center with a teaspoon of the tuna mixture, leaving a ½-inch (1 cm) border of rice around the edges.

5. Add another 2 tablespoons of rice on top of the tuna mixture to cover. Press the top cover of the mold to shape it all together.

6. Heat a large nonstick or cast-iron pan over medium heat and add enough vegetable oil to coat the bottom of the pan. Place the onigiri in the pan and cook until golden brown and crispy, 4 to 5 minutes per side.

7. Remove from the heat and carefully wrap each onigiri with a strip of nori halfway down from one side to the other. Adhere the nori with water. Serve warm.

SUNOMONO
(CUCUMBER SALAD)

15 minutes
Prep time

30 minutes
Chill Time

45 minutes
Total Time

Level: ★☆☆☆

Serves 4

INGREDIENTS

Kosher salt

2 medium Persian cucumbers, thinly sliced (see Tip)

2 tablespoons rice vinegar

1 tablespoon soy sauce

1 tablespoon sugar

1 teaspoon sesame oil

TOPPINGS (OPTIONAL)

Sesame seeds

Shredded seaweed (nori)

1. In a colander set in the sink, sprinkle a pinch of salt over the cucumber slices and let them sit for about 10 minutes to draw out moisture.

2. Gently squeeze the cucumbers and pat them dry with a paper towel to remove any excess moisture.

3. In a small bowl, mix the vinegar, soy sauce, sugar, sesame oil, and ¼ teaspoon salt until the sugar has dissolved.

4. Place the cucumber slices in a large bowl and pour the dressing over them. Toss well to coat.

5. Cover the bowl and refrigerate for at least 30 minutes to allow the flavors to meld.

6. Before serving, sprinkle some sesame seeds and/or shredded seaweed on top for added flavor and presentation, if desired.

TIP: Use a mandolin for thin, even slices.

GARLIC SOY EDAMAME

5 minutes
Prep time

10 minutes
Cook Time

15 minutes
Total Time

Level: ★☆☆☆

Serves 4

INGREDIENTS

1 pound (454 g) edamame (frozen or fresh)

1 tablespoon sesame oil

3 garlic cloves, minced

2 tablespoons soy sauce

½ teaspoon red pepper flakes, optional

Kosher salt

1. If using frozen edamame, cook according to package directions. If using fresh edamame, blanch in boiling water until tender, about 5 minutes, then cool in an ice bath. Drain and set aside.

2. In a large pan or skillet, heat the sesame oil over medium heat. Add the garlic to the pan and sauté until fragrant, about 1 minute.

3. Add the edamame and stir-fry until heated through, 2 to 3 minutes.

4. Drizzle the soy sauce over the edamame and toss to coat. If desired, sprinkle in the red pepper flakes for some extra heat.

5. Cook, stirring occasionally, until the edamame is well coated with the soy sauce, 1 to 2 more minutes. Remove from the heat and serve hot.

JAPAN:
GYUDON BEEF RICE BOWL + KABOCHA SQUASH TEMPURA + MISO SOUP

This Japanese lunch includes a gyudon beef rice bowl, where tender beef strips are bathed in a savory sauce that perfectly melts into the rice underneath. Pack a medium-boiled egg on the side to add to the top of the gyudon. Serve with kabocha squash tempura, slices of sweet and crispy squash with tempura dipping sauce. Sip on comforting miso soup, brimming with tofu, mushrooms, and green onions.

MISO SOUP

10 minutes
Prep time

20 minutes
Cook Time

30 minutes
Total Time

Level: ★☆☆☆

Serves 4

×

INGREDIENTS

½ cup (70 g) sliced shiitake, cremini, or button mushrooms

1 cup (200 g) diced silken or firm tofu

1 sheet seaweed, optional

3 to 4 tablespoons white or red miso paste

⅓ cup (34 g) chopped green onions

1 teaspoon soy sauce, optional

1. Bring 4 cups (960 ml) of water to a boil in a medium pot.

2. Reduce the heat to low and add the mushrooms, tofu, and seaweed (if using). Let simmer until the mushrooms are tender, about 5 minutes.

3. In a small bowl, whisk the miso paste with a few tablespoons of hot soup broth until smooth. Add the mixture to the pot and stir well to combine. Simmer for another 2 to 3 minutes (see Tip), then remove from heat and add the green onions.

4. Taste the soup and adjust the seasoning if needed. Add the soy sauce for extra flavor, if desired.

5. Serve hot and enjoy!

TIP: Don't let the soup boil after adding the miso paste, as high heat can destroy some of miso's beneficial enzymes.

GYUDON BEEF RICE BOWL

10 minutes
Prep time

25 minutes
Cook Time

35 minutes
Total Time

Level: ★★☆☆

Serves 4

1. In a large skillet, heat the oil over medium heat. Add the onions and cook until translucent and lightly caramelized, 7 to 8 minutes.

2. Push the onions to one side of the pan and add the beef. Cook, stirring occasionally, until browned on all sides, about 5 minutes.

3. In a small bowl, mix the dashi, soy sauce, mirin, sake, and sugar. Pour the mixture into the pan.

4. Bring to a simmer and cook until the flavors meld together and the beef is cooked through, about 5 minutes. Remove from the heat.

5. Serve the beef over a bowl of rice.

6. Garnish with green onions, pickled ginger, soft-boiled egg, and sesame seeds, if desired.

NOTE: I don't like packing soft-boiled eggs in lunches, as they can be messy. If packing this for lunch, swap out the soft-boiled egg for a medium-boiled one.

INGREDIENTS

2 tablespoons vegetable oil

2 yellow onions, thinly sliced

1 pound (454 g) boneless ribeye steak, thinly sliced

1 cup (240 ml) dashi stock

3 tablespoons soy sauce

2 tablespoons mirin (Japanese sweet rice wine)

2 tablespoons sake (Japanese rice wine)

2 tablespoons sugar

4 cups (800 g) cooked short-grain white rice

TOPPINGS (OPTIONAL)

Chopped green onions

Pickled ginger

Soft-boiled egg

Sesame seeds

KABOCHA SQUASH TEMPURA

15 minutes
Prep time

25 minutes
Cook Time

40 minutes
Total Time

Level: ★★☆☆   **Serves 4 to 6**

1. Halve the squash and remove the seeds. Peel the skin off and cut the flesh into thin slices, about ½-inch (1cm) thick.

2. In a large pan, heat ½ inch (1cm) vegetable oil to 350°F (175°C).

3. In a medium bowl, combine the all-purpose flour, cornstarch, baking powder, and salt.

4. Gradually add ice-cold water while whisking, until you achieve a thin, smooth batter. Be careful not to overmix.

5. Dip the kabocha slices into the batter, ensuring they are fully coated.

6. Carefully place the kabocha slices into the oil, a few at a time, and fry until golden brown and crispy, 3 to 4 minutes per side.

7. Use a slotted spoon or tongs to remove the tempura from the oil and transfer to a paper towel–lined plate to drain.

8. Repeat the process with the remaining kabocha, ensuring the oil temperature stays consistent, and removing any stray bits of cooked batter with a slotted spoon between batches.

9. Serve immediately with tempura dipping sauce (and grated radish and ginger, if desired) on the side. Cool completely when packing into a lunch.

INGREDIENTS

1 small kabocha squash
Vegetable oil
1 cup (120 g) all-purpose flour
½ cup (60 g) cornstarch
1 teaspoon baking powder
½ teaspoon kosher salt

FOR SERVING

Tempura dipping sauce (tentsuyu)
Grated daikon radish, optional
Grated ginger, optional

FRANCE:
MINI RATATOUILLE + MADELEINES

For today's lunch, we are going to France! This mini ratatouille is full of vegetables—eggplant, zucchini, bell peppers, and tomatoes—seasoned with aromatic herbs for a burst of flavor. And for a treat: freshly baked madeleines. I always loved madeleines growing up, but I could rarely find them. Now, I make them whenever I want! For sides, this lunch has dried apricots, granola, and a medley of berries.

MINI RATATOUILLE

20 minutes
Prep time

40 minutes
Cook Time

1 hour
Total Time

Level: ★★★☆	Serves 4

1. Preheat the oven to 375°F (190°C).

2. Heat 2 tablespoons of olive oil in a large skillet over medium heat. Add the onion, bell peppers, and garlic and sauté until translucent, 2 to 3 minutes.

3. Add the tomatoes, thyme, salt, and black pepper to taste. Stir well and let simmer for about 5 minutes.

4. Meanwhile, brush four mini baking dishes (or one 9 x 13-inch/ 23 x 33 cm baking dish) with olive oil.

5. Arrange the eggplant, zucchini, and yellow squash slices in alternating patterns in the baking dishes.

6. Drizzle the remaining 2 tablespoons olive oil over the vegetables and season with salt and black pepper.

7. Pour the tomato sauce evenly over the vegetables, making sure to cover them completely.

8. Cover the baking dish with aluminum foil and bake for 30 to 35 minutes, until the vegetables are tender.

9. Remove the foil and continue baking for an additional 10 minutes to allow the top to brown slightly.

10. Garnish with fresh basil leaves before serving.

INGREDIENTS

4 tablespoons olive oil, divided, plus more for greasing

1 small onion, chopped

1 red bell pepper, chopped

1 yellow bell pepper, chopped

3 garlic cloves, minced

1 cup (240 g) crushed tomatoes

1 teaspoon dried thyme

Kosher salt and black pepper

2 to 3 baby eggplants, thinly sliced

1 small zucchini, thinly sliced

1 small yellow squash, thinly sliced

Fresh basil leaves

TOOLS

Four 5.75 x 3-inch (15 x 7 cm) loaf pans (for minis) or one 9 x 13-inch (23 x 33 cm) baking dish

Aluminum foil

MADELEINES

75 minutes
(with chill time)
Prep time

12 minutes
Cook Time

87 minutes
Total Time

Level: ★★★☆

Makes 8 to 12

1. In a small bowl, whisk together the flour, baking powder, and salt. Set aside.

2. In a large bowl, beat together the granulated sugar and butter until well combined.

3. Add the eggs, one at a time, beating well after each addition. Stir in the vanilla extract and lemon zest, if desired.

4. Gradually fold in the dry ingredients into the wet mixture, stirring gently until just combined. Do not overmix.

5. Cover the batter and refrigerate for at least 1 hour or overnight to chill and develop flavor.

6. Preheat the oven to 375°F (190°C). Grease a madeleine pan with cooking spray.

7. Spoon about 1 tablespoon of batter into each madeleine mold, filling them about three quarters of the way full.

8. Bake for 10 to 12 minutes, until the madeleines are golden brown around the edges and spring back when lightly pressed.

9. Remove from the oven and let the madeleines cool in the pan for a few minutes. Transfer them to a wire rack to cool completely.

10. Lightly dust the madeleines with powdered sugar before serving.

INGREDIENTS

⅔ cup (80 g) all-purpose flour

½ teaspoon baking powder

Pinch of kosher salt

⅔ cup (133 g) granulated sugar

8 tablespoons unsalted butter, melted and cooled

2 large eggs

1 teaspoon vanilla extract

Zest of 1 lemon, optional

Nonstick cooking spray

Powdered sugar

TOOLS

Madeleine pan

Wire rack

"Mr. Brightside" — **The Killers**

You are my
happy place.

AUSTRALIA:

CHICKEN PARMA
+ FAIRY BREAD

This delicious Australian-inspired lunch features chicken parma, fairy bread, and corn on the cob. Enjoy the crispy chicken topped with flavorful tomato sauce, savor the whimsical and crunchy sprinkles on the soft bread, and delight in the buttery corn: an unforgettable combination! For snacks and sides, add in Tim Tams, kiwi, blueberries, and clementines.

CHICKEN PARMA

15 minutes	**30 minutes**	**45 minutes**
Prep time	Cook Time	Total Time

Level: ★★★☆	Serves 4

1. Preheat your oven to 400°F (200°C).

2. Season the chicken with salt and pepper on both sides.

3. Set up a breading station: Place the flour in one shallow dish, the beaten eggs in another dish, and the bread crumbs in a third dish.

4. Coat each chicken breast in the flour, shaking off any excess. Then dip it into the beaten eggs, allowing any excess to drip off. Finally, coat the chicken in the bread crumbs, pressing them in gently to ensure they adhere well.

5. Heat about ¼ inch (6 mm) of vegetable oil in a large skillet over medium heat. Fry the chicken until golden brown and cooked through, 3 to 4 minutes per side. Remove from the skillet and place on a paper towel–lined plate.

6. Transfer the chicken to a baking dish. Top each filet with a slice of ham, followed by a slice of mozzarella.

7. Pour the marinara sauce evenly over the chicken.

8. Bake for 15 to 20 minutes, until the cheese is melted.

9. Remove from the oven and garnish with grated Parmesan and fresh basil leaves.

10. Serve hot.

INGREDIENTS

4 chicken breasts

Kosher salt and black pepper

1 cup (120 ml) all-purpose flour

2 eggs, beaten

2 cups (220 g) bread crumbs

Vegetable oil

4 slices ham

4 slices mozzarella

1 cup (240 ml) marinara sauce

Grated Parmesan

Fresh basil leaves, sliced

TOOLS

Baking dish

FAIRY BREAD

10 minutes
Prep time

0 minutes
Cook Time

10 minutes
Total Time

Level: ★☆☆☆

Serves 1

1. Spread the butter onto the entire surface of the bread slice.

2. Pour the sprinkles into a shallow bowl or plate.

3. Press the buttered side of the bread slice into the bowl of sprinkles, making sure they stick to the butter.

4. Lift the bread slice from the sprinkles, allowing any excess to fall back into the bowl.

5. Cut the slice of fairy bread diagonally or into smaller rectangles, if desired. Serve immediately and enjoy!

NOTE: Fairy bread is typically served at children's birthday parties or as a fun treat.

INGREDIENTS ✕

1 slice white bread

1 tablespoon unsalted butter, softened

Rainbow sprinkles (hundreds and thousands)

ITALY:
ANTIPASTO SKEWERS + MUSHROOM ARANCINI + TIRAMISU

Experience the flavors of Italy with cute antipasto skewers, mushroom and rice arancini, and tiramisu. These little mozzarella and tomato skewers make for a perfect bite. The crispy arancini filled with mushrooms are truly decadent. Indulge in this tiramisu, with layers of ladyfingers soaked in coffee and creamy mascarpone. *Buon appetito!*

ANTIPASTO SKEWERS

15 minutes
Prep time

0 minutes
Cook Time

15 minutes
Total Time

Level: ★☆☆☆

Makes 10

×

INGREDIENTS

10 black olives

10 basil leaves

10 slices salami or pepperoni

10 mini fresh mozzarella balls

10 cherry tomatoes

TOOLS

Ten 4- to 6-inch (10 to 15 cm) skewers or food picks

1. Thread an olive onto a skewer, followed by a basil leaf, a folded slice of salami or pepperoni, a mozzarella ball, and a tomato.

2. Repeat with the remaining skewers and ingredients.

3. Serve immediately and enjoy!

NOTE: Feel free to customize your antipasto skewers by adding other ingredients, such as roasted red peppers, grilled zucchini, or pickled onions.

MUSHROOM ARANCINI

30 minutes
Prep time

30 minutes
Cook Time

1 hour
Total Time

Level: ★★★☆

Makes 12

INGREDIENTS

2½ cups (600 ml) vegetable broth

2½ tablespoons olive oil, divided

1 small onion, finely chopped

2 garlic cloves, minced

1 cup (200 g) Arborio rice

8 ounces (227 g) porcini, cremini, or button mushrooms, finely chopped

½ cup (50 g) grated Parmesan

Kosher salt and black pepper

2 large eggs, beaten

Bread crumbs, for coating

Vegetable oil, for frying

Chopped parsley, for garnish

1. In a small saucepan, bring the vegetable broth to a simmer over medium heat.

2. In a large saucepan, heat 1 tablespoon olive oil over medium heat. Add the onion and garlic and sauté until translucent, 2 to 3 minutes.

3. Add the rice and stir for about 1 minute, allowing the rice to toast slightly.

4. Add the simmering vegetable broth to the rice mixture, one ladleful at a time. Stir continuously until each ladle of liquid is absorbed before adding the next. Continue until all the broth has been added and absorbed and the rice is al dente, about 20 minutes. Remove from the heat.

5. Stir in the Parmesan and season with salt and pepper if needed. Let cool slightly.

6. In another medium pan, heat 1½ tablespoons olive oil over medium heat. Add the mushrooms and sauté until they release their moisture and are golden brown, 5 to 7 minutes. Season with salt and pepper to taste. Remove from the heat.

7. Divide the rice into 12 portions, then flatten each one in your palm. Place a spoonful of sautéed mushrooms into the center of each rice ball and shape the rice around it.

8. Dip each rice ball into the beaten eggs, ensuring they are fully coated. Roll them in bread crumbs, making sure they are evenly coated.

9. To a large pot, add enough vegetable oil to submerge the rice balls. Heat to 350°F (175°C). Carefully add the rice balls into the hot oil and fry until golden brown, 3 to 4 minutes. Use a slotted spoon to transfer them to paper towels to drain any excess oil.

10. Garnish with parsley and serve warm.

TIRAMISU

20 minutes Prep time	**4 hours** Chill Time	**4 hours and 20 minutes** Total Time

Level: ★★☆☆　　　　　　　　　　　　　　　**Serves 12**

1. In a medium bowl, whisk together the egg yolks and sugar until creamy.
2. In a small saucepan, heat the milk over medium heat until it starts to simmer.
3. Slowly pour the hot milk into the egg yolk mixture, whisking continuously to prevent curdling.
4. Return the mixture to the saucepan and cook over low heat, stirring constantly, until it thickens and coats the back of a spoon, 5 to 7 minutes. Remove from the heat and let the mixture cool completely.
5. In a small bowl, beat the heavy cream until stiff peaks form.
6. In a large bowl, whip the mascarpone until creamy, 1 to 2 minutes. Fold in the custard mixture and vanilla, then gently fold in the whipped cream.
7. Dip each ladyfinger into the coffee for a few seconds, allowing them to soak up some liquid but not become too soggy.
8. Arrange half of the soaked ladyfingers in a single layer in the bottom of a 9 x 13-inch (23 x 33 cm) serving dish.
9. Spread half of the mascarpone mixture over the ladyfingers in an even layer.
10. Repeat the process with the remaining ladyfingers and mascarpone.
11. Cover the dish with plastic wrap and refrigerate for at least 4 hours or overnight to allow the tiramisu to set.
12. Just before serving, dust the top with cocoa powder and top with mint leaves. Slice and serve chilled.

×

INGREDIENTS

6 egg yolks

¾ cup (150 g) sugar

⅔ cup (160 ml) milk

1¼ cups (300 ml) heavy cream

8 ounces (227 g) mascarpone

1 teaspoon vanilla extract

1 cup (240 ml) brewed coffee or espresso, cooled (I use decaf for kids)

40 ladyfingers

Cocoa powder, for garnish

Mint leaves, for garnish

"Do not wait for someone else to come and speak for you. It's you who can change the world."

—MALALA YOUSAFZAI

GERMANY:
KARTOFFELKLOESSE + SAVORY GRAVY + BRAISED CABBAGE WITH APPLES

Experience the wonderful flavors of Germany with this lunch featuring Kartoffelkloesse, soft and pillowy potato dumplings, served with a rich, savory gravy. Accompanying these delicious dumplings is a sweet and tender braised cabbage with apples. Immerse yourself in this hearty dish, as every bite transports you to Germany.

"Shelter" — **Porter Robinson & Madeon**

KARTOFFELKLOESSE
(POTATO DUMPLINGS)

15 minutes
Prep time

35 minutes
Cook Time

50 minutes
Total Time

Level: ★★★☆	Makes 8 to 10

1. Peel the potatoes, then place them in a large pot. Cover with cold water. Bring to a boil and cook until soft, about 20 minutes. Drain and let cool slightly.

2. Pass the potatoes through a potato ricer or shred with a cheese grater.

3. In a large bowl, combine the potatoes, flour, eggs, salt, and nutmeg. Mix well to form a dough.

4. Bring a pot of salted water to a simmer over medium heat.

5. Divide the dough into 8 to 10 equal portions. Roll each portion into a ball and flatten slightly.

6. Gently drop the dumplings into the simmering water, being careful not to overcrowd the pot. Cook in batches.

7. Simmer until they are cooked through and start to float to the surface, 10 to 15 minutes.

8. Using a slotted spoon, transfer the dumplings to a serving dish.

9. Serve hot with gravy, braised cabbage, and sauerkraut, if desired.

INGREDIENTS

5 medium russet potatoes

½ cup (60 g) all-purpose flour

2 eggs

1 teaspoon kosher salt

¼ teaspoon ground nutmeg

FOR SERVING

Savory Gravy (page 249)

Braised Cabbage with Apples (page 249)

Sauerkraut

TOOLS

Potato ricer or cheese grater

SAVORY GRAVY

5 minutes
Prep time

15 minutes
Cook Time

20 minutes
Total Time

Level: ★☆☆☆

Makes 2 cups (480ml)

INGREDIENTS

3 tablespoons butter

3 tablespoons all-purpose flour

2 cups (480 ml) beef broth

½ cup (120 ml) heavy cream

Kosher salt and black pepper

1. In a medium saucepan, melt the butter over medium heat.
2. Add the flour and whisk continuously until it forms a roux (a smooth paste). Cook for about 2 minutes, stirring constantly.
3. Gradually pour in the broth, whisking vigorously to prevent lumps.
4. Bring to a simmer and cook until the gravy thickens, stirring occasionally, 5 to 7 minutes.
5. Stir in the heavy cream and cook for another 2 to 3 minutes. Season with salt and pepper to taste.
6. Remove the gravy from heat and let rest for a few minutes to thicken further.
7. Serve hot alongside Kartoffelkloesse.

BRAISED CABBAGE WITH APPLES

15 minutes
Prep time

40 minutes
Cook Time

55 minutes
Total Time

Level: ★☆☆☆

Serves 4 to 6

INGREDIENTS

3 tablespoons butter

1 large onion, thinly sliced

1 medium head of cabbage, shredded

2 apples, peeled and sliced

2 tablespoons brown sugar

1 cup (240 ml) vegetable or chicken broth

¼ cup (60 ml) apple cider vinegar

Kosher salt and black pepper

1. In a large pot or Dutch oven, melt the butter over medium heat.
2. Add the onions and cook until they become translucent and start to caramelize, about 5 minutes.
3. Stir in the cabbage and apples, then sprinkle with brown sugar. Cook for another 5 minutes, stirring occasionally to coat everything evenly.
4. Pour in the broth and vinegar. Season with salt and pepper to taste.
5. Reduce the heat to low, cover, and simmer until the cabbage is tender, stirring occasionally, 30 to 40 minutes.
6. Adjust the seasoning if needed and serve hot.

UNITED KINGDOM:

DECONSTRUCTED COTTAGE PIE + ONION GRAVY + LEMON & CHERRY MINI BUNDT CAKES

Experience the taste of Britain with this deconstructed cottage pie. Enjoy layers of flavorful minced meat, creamy mashed potatoes, and tender vegetables. Drizzle the pie with some savory onion gravy to enhance the rich flavors. For something sweet, try this delightful lemon and cherry mini bundt cake, a perfect balance of zesty lemon and sweet cherries. Cheers!

ONION GRAVY

10 minutes
Prep time

30 minutes
Cook Time

40 minutes
Total Time

Level: ★☆☆☆

Makes 2 cups (480 ml)

INGREDIENTS

2 large onions, thinly sliced

2 tablespoons butter or vegetable oil

2 tablespoons all-purpose flour

2 cups (480 ml) beef or vegetable broth

1 teaspoon Worcestershire sauce

Kosher salt and black pepper

1. In a large skillet, melt the butter over medium heat. Add the onions and sauté until soft and caramelized, 15 to 20 minutes. Stir occasionally to prevent burning.

2. Sprinkle the flour over the onions and stir well to coat. Cook for another minute.

3. Gradually pour in the broth, whisking constantly to avoid lumps. Add the Worcestershire sauce and season with salt and pepper to taste.

4. Reduce the heat to low and simmer for 10 to 15 minutes, stirring occasionally, until the gravy thickens to your desired consistency.

5. For a smoother consistency, blend the gravy using an immersion blender or transfer it to a regular blender. (Be careful when blending hot liquids.) Adjust the seasoning if necessary.

6. Serve the onion gravy alongside roasted meats, mashed potatoes, or other dishes of your choice.

DECONSTRUCTED COTTAGE PIE

15 minutes
Prep time

30 minutes
Cook Time

45 minutes
Total Time

Level: ★★☆☆

Serves 4

1. In a large skillet, cook the ground beef over medium heat until browned. Drain any excess fat.

2. Add the onion, carrots, and garlic and cook until softened, 5 to 7 minutes.

3. Stir in the beef broth, tomato paste, Worcestershire sauce, salt, and pepper. Simmer for 10 to 15 minutes, until the mixture thickens.

4. To serve, spoon a generous portion of mashed potatoes into each bowl. Top with the beef mixture.

5. Top with onion gravy, garnish with parsley, and serve hot.

INGREDIENTS

1 pound (454 g) ground beef

1 yellow onion, chopped

2 medium carrots, diced

2 garlic cloves, minced

1 cup (240 ml) beef broth

2 tablespoons tomato paste

1 tablespoon Worcestershire sauce

Kosher salt and black pepper

4 cups (900 g) Butter Mashed Potatoes (page 39)

Onion Gravy (page 251), for serving

Chopped parsley, for garnish

LEMON & CHERRY MINI BUNDT CAKES

15 minutes
Prep time

20 minutes
Cook Time

30 minutes
Cooling time

1 hour 5 minutes
Total Time

Level: ★★★☆

Makes 6 cakes

1. Preheat the oven to 350°F (175°C). Grease your cake pan with butter.

2. Reserve 2 tablespoons of flour, then add the remaining flour to a medium bowl and whisk in the baking powder and salt. Set aside.

3. In a large bowl, cream together the butter and granulated sugar until light and fluffy.

4. Add the eggs one at a time, beating well after each addition. Mix in the vanilla, lemon zest, and lemon juice.

5. Gradually add the dry ingredients to the wet ingredients, alternating with the milk. Begin and end with the dry ingredients. Mix until just combined.

6. In a small bowl, coat the cherries with the reserved 2 tablespoons of flour. Gently fold the cherries into the batter.

7. Spoon the batter into the cake pan, filling each cavity about two-thirds full.

8. Bake for about 20 minutes, until a toothpick inserted into the center of each cake comes out clean.

9. Remove from the oven and let the cakes cool in the pan for about 10 minutes. Transfer to a wire rack to cool completely.

10. Make the glaze: In a small bowl, whisk together the powdered sugar and lemon juice until smooth. Adjust the consistency by adding more lemon juice if needed.

11. Drizzle the glaze over the cakes and sprinkle with lemon zest. Allow the glaze to set before serving.

INGREDIENTS

8 tablespoons unsalted butter, softened, plus more for greasing

1¾ cups (210 g) all-purpose flour, divided

1½ teaspoons baking powder

¼ teaspoon kosher salt

1 cup (200 g) granulated sugar

2 large eggs

1 teaspoon vanilla extract

Zest and juice of 1 lemon

½ cup (120 ml) milk

1 cup (150 g) fresh or frozen cherries, pitted and roughly chopped

GLAZE

1 cup (120 g) powdered sugar

2 to 3 tablespoons lemon juice

Lemon zest

TOOLS

Six-cavity mini Bundt cake pan

Parchment paper

Wire rack

COOKING STAPLES

STEAMED RICE

5 minutes
Prep time

20 minutes
Cook Time

25 minutes
Total Time

Level: ★☆☆☆

Makes 6 cups (1.1 kg)

INGREDIENTS ✕

2 cups (400 g)
   long-grain white
   rice

1. Place the rice in a fine-mesh strainer and rinse it under cold running water for 1 to 2 minutes until the water runs clear, to remove excess starch

2. If you have time, soak the rice 15 to 30 minutes. This softens the rice and makes it fluffier. Drain before cooking.

3. In a medium saucepan with a tight-fitting lid, combine the rinsed rice and 2½ cups (600 ml) water.

4. Bring to a boil, then reduce the heat to low and cover. Simmer for about 15 minutes, until the rice is tender and the water is absorbed.

5. Turn off the heat but keep the saucepan covered. Let the rice sit undisturbed for 5 minutes to steam.

6. Remove the lid and fluff the rice gently with a fork or rice scooper to separate the grains.

NOTE: The cooking time may vary slightly depending on the type of rice and your stovetop. It's important not to lift the lid or stir the rice during the cooking process to ensure even steaming.

PERFECT BOILED EGGS

5 minutes
Prep time

4 to 12 minutes
Cook Time

14 to 22 minutes
with cooling time
Total Time

Level: ★☆☆☆

Makes as many as you'd like

INGREDIENTS

Eggs

1. Fill a medium pot with enough water to cover the eggs completely. Bring the water to a rolling boil.

2. Gently lower the eggs into the boiling water, using a slotted spoon to prevent them from cracking.

3. Reduce the heat slightly to maintain a gentle boil.

4. Cook the eggs for the desired amount of time:
   Soft-boiled eggs: 5 to 6 minutes
   Medium-boiled eggs: 7 to 8 minutes
   Hard-boiled eggs: 9 to 12 minutes

5. Transfer the eggs to a bowl of ice water to stop the cooking process. Let the eggs cool for a few minutes before peeling.

TIP: I like to peel the eggs under cold running water to help loosen the shell and make it easier to remove.

OAT MILK

5 minutes
Prep time

0 minutes
Cook Time

5 minutes
Total Time

| Level: ★☆☆☆ | Makes 4 cups (960 ml) |

INGREDIENTS

1 cup (90 g) rolled oats

Sweetener (such as maple syrup, honey, or dates), optional

Flavoring (such as vanilla extract or cinnamon), optional

Pinch of salt

TOOLS

Blender or food processor

Nut milk bag, cheesecloth, or fine mesh strainer, optional

---

1. Rinse the oats thoroughly under running water to remove any debris.

2. Add the oats and 4 cups (960 ml) water to a blender or food processor.

3. Blend on high speed until the mixture becomes smooth and creamy, 30 to 60 seconds.

4. If desired, strain the mixture using a nut milk bag, cheesecloth, or fine mesh strainer to remove any remaining solids.

5. Return the strained milk to the blender and add any sweeteners or flavorings, if desired, and the salt. Blend again briefly to incorporate.

6. Taste and adjust the sweetness or flavorings as desired.

7. Transfer to a clean glass jar or bottle and refrigerate for 3 to 4 days.

NOTE: Homemade oat milk may naturally separate in the refrigerator, so give it a good shake or stir before using it.

ALMOND MILK

5 minutes
Prep time

0 minutes
Cook Time

8 hours
with soaking time
Total Time

| Level: ★☆☆☆ | Makes 4 cups (960 ml) |

INGREDIENTS

1 cup (140 g) raw almonds

Sweetener (such as dates, maple syrup, or honey), optional

Flavoring (such as vanilla extract or cinnamon), optional

Pinch of salt

TOOLS

Blender or food processor

Nut milk bag, cheesecloth, or fine mesh strainer, optional

---

1. Place the almonds in a bowl and cover them with water. Soak for at least 8 hours or overnight.

2. Drain and rinse thoroughly under running water.

3. Add the almonds and 4 cups (960 ml) of fresh water to a blender or food processor.

4. Blend on high speed until creamy and smooth, 1 to 2 minutes.

5. If desired, strain the mixture using a nut milk bag, cheesecloth, or fine mesh strainer to remove any remaining solids.

6. Return the strained milk to the blender and add any sweeteners or flavorings, if desired, and the salt. Blend again briefly to incorporate.

7. Taste and adjust the sweetness or flavorings as desired.

8. Transfer to a clean glass jar or bottle and refrigerate for 3 to 4 days.

NOTE: Homemade almond milk may naturally separate in the refrigerator, so give it a good shake or stir before using it.

VEGETABLE STOCK

15 minutes
Prep time

2 hours
Cook Time

2 hours and 15 minutes
Total Time

Level: ★☆☆☆

Makes 6 to 8 cups (1.5 to 2 L)

INGREDIENTS

2 onions, roughly chopped

3 carrots, roughly chopped

3 celery stalks, roughly chopped

1 leek, sliced, optional

5 garlic cloves, smashed

1 bay leaf

Fresh herbs (such as parsley, thyme, or rosemary), optional

Kosher salt and black pepper

TOOLS

Fine mesh sieve or cheesecloth

1. To a large pot, add the onions, carrots, celery, leek (if using), garlic, bay leaf, and any desired fresh herbs. Season with salt and pepper to taste.
2. Pour enough water into the pot to cover all the ingredients and bring to a boil over medium-high heat.
3. Reduce the heat to low and simmer for 1 to 2 hours.
4. Remove from the heat and let cool slightly.
5. Strain the liquid through a fine-mesh sieve or cheesecloth into another pot or container, discarding the solids.
6. Let cool completely before storing in airtight containers in the refrigerator for 4 to 5 days or in the freezer for 6 months.

NOTE: You can also add other vegetables like mushrooms, bell peppers, or tomatoes to enhance the flavor. Feel free to adjust the quantities of vegetables, herbs, and seasonings to your preference.

CHICKEN STOCK

10 minutes
Prep time

3 hours
Cook Time

3 hours and 10 minutes
Total Time

Level: ★☆☆☆

Makes about 12 cups (3 L)

INGREDIENTS

One whole chicken (leftover from roasted chicken or raw)

2 carrots, roughly chopped

2 celery stalks, roughly chopped

1 onion, peeled and quartered

6 garlic cloves, smashed

Fresh herbs (such as parsley, thyme, or bay leaves), optional

Kosher salt and black pepper

TOOLS

Fine mesh sieve or cheesecloth

1. If using a leftover roasted chicken, remove any excess meat from the bones. If using a raw chicken, leave the meat on.

2. To a large pot, add the chicken, carrots, celery, onion, garlic, and fresh herbs. Season with salt and pepper to taste.

3. Pour enough water into the pot to cover all the ingredients and bring to a boil over medium-high heat.

4. Reduce the heat to low and simmer for 2 to 3 hours. Skim off any foam or impurities that rise to the surface.

5. Remove from the heat and let cool slightly.

6. Remove the chicken from the pot and reserve any meat for another use. Strain the liquid through a fine mesh sieve or cheesecloth into another pot or container, discarding the solids.

7. Let cool completely before storing in airtight containers in the refrigerator for 4 to 5 days or in the freezer for up to 6 months.

BEEF BONE BROTH

10 minutes
Prep time

4 hours
Cook Time

4 hours and 10 minutes
Total Time

Level: ★☆☆☆

Makes 9 cups (2 L)

INGREDIENTS

2½ pounds (1 kg) beef bones
(marrow or knuckle bones)

1 large onion, peeled and quartered

3 garlic cloves, crushed

One 2-inch (5 cm) piece of ginger,
sliced

1 teaspoon kosher salt, or to taste

1 small Korean radish (mu) or daikon
radish, sliced into thick rounds,
optional

TOOLS

Fine mesh sieve or cheesecloth

1. Preheat your oven to 450°F (230°C). Place the beef bones on a baking sheet and roast for about 30 minutes until browned.

2. To a large pot, add the beef bones, onion, garlic, ginger, salt, and radish, if using. Cover with 9 cups (2 L) water.

3. Bring to a boil over high heat, then reduce the heat to medium-low and simmer for 2 hours. Skim off any impurities or foam that rise to the surface. Add more water if it has reduced too much and simmer for another 1 to 2 hours.

4. Strain the broth using a fine-mesh sieve or cheesecloth, discarding the solids. You should be left with a clear and flavorful bone broth. Taste and adjust the salt if needed.

5. Let cool completely before storing in airtight containers in the refrigerator for 4 to 5 days or in the freezer for 6 months.

FRUIT CHIPS

10 minutes
Prep time

3 minutes
Cook Time

3 hours and 10 minutes
Total Time

Level: ★☆☆☆

Makes as many as you'd like

INGREDIENTS

Fresh fruits, such as apples,
bananas, strawberries,
or pineapples

Lemon juice, optional

TOOLS

Baking sheet

Parchment paper

Mandoline

1. Preheat your oven to 225°F (110°C) and line a baking sheet with parchment paper.

2. Wash and dry the fruits thoroughly, then thinly slice using a mandoline or sharp knife.

3. Lightly coat the sliced fruits in lemon juice to prevent browning, if desired. (I recommend this for apples and bananas.)

4. Arrange the fruit slices on the baking sheet in a single layer, ensuring they do not overlap.

5. Bake for 2 to 3 hours, until the fruits are crisp and completely dried. Keep an eye on them toward the end to ensure they don't burn.

6. Remove from the oven and let cool completely on the baking sheet. They will become crispier as they cool down.

7. Store in an airtight container for up to a week. Enjoy as a healthy snack!

NOTE: Baking time may vary depending on the thickness and moisture content of the fruits. Thinner slices will dry faster than thicker ones. Adjust the baking time accordingly.

VEGGIE CHIPS

10 minutes
Prep time

15 minutes
Cook Time

25 minutes
Total Time

Level: ★☆☆☆

Makes as many as you'd like

INGREDIENTS

Assorted vegetables, such as sweet potatoes, beets, carrots, zucchini, or kale

Olive oil

Kosher salt

Seasonings, such as paprika, garlic powder, ground cumin, or dried herbs

TOOLS

Baking sheet

Parchment paper

Mandoline

Wire rack

1. Preheat your oven to 350°F (180°C) and line a baking sheet with parchment paper.

2. Wash and dry the vegetables thoroughly. Peel them, if desired, or leave the skin on for added nutrition and texture.

3. Slice the vegetables into very thin slices using a mandoline or a sharp knife. Make the slices as uniform as possible to ensure even cooking.

4. Place the vegetables in a large bowl and drizzle a few tablespoons of olive oil over them. Toss gently to coat .

5. Sprinkle salt and any other seasonings onto the vegetables. Mix well to evenly distribute the seasonings.

6. Arrange the vegetable slices in a single layer on the baking sheet, making sure they do not overlap.

7. Bake for 12 to 15 minutes, until the edges of the chips are golden brown and the chips are crispy. Keep a close eye on them, as they can quickly go from crisp to burnt.

8. Remove from the oven and let the chips cool completely on a wire rack.

9. Store in an airtight container at room temperature for up to a week.

INDEX

ACKNOWLEDGMENTS

THANK YOU to my dedicated followers and fans. I am deeply honored by all of your support and encouragement. You all have been the driving force behind my journey as a content creator and author. You have inspired me to explore my culinary creativity and share it with the world. Your kind words have motivated me to push my boundaries and create something truly special in this cookbook. I am incredibly fortunate to have such an amazing community that allows me to be myself and embrace my passion. This book would not have been possible without you, and I am forever grateful for your presence in my life.

To my beloved baby girls, your love has been a constant source of strength throughout this entire journey. Your understanding and willingness to let me work and rest when needed have been invaluable. Thank you for always being there for me and for being the best part of my life. Thank you for making me the person I am today.

A big thank you to my little sister Omi. From the very beginning, you have been my number one supporter, consistently encouraging me to make videos. Your belief in me has been a driving force behind my creative endeavors, and I am grateful for your constant motivation.

My daddy. Your love, guidance, and support has been instrumental in shaping me into the person I am today. Your belief in my abilities and opportunities to grow have given me the confidence to pursue my dreams. Thank you for showing me how to love in different ways and inspiring my love for photography and videography. Thank you for everything you have done for me.

To my stepmom, for your guidance and teaching me how to cook Filipino food and fostering a shared love of cooking. Your support has been a constant source of encouragement.

이모, who helped raise me and is a second mom to me. 고마워요

Mara and Osoo, for being the best little sisters anyone could ask for. Your love and support have meant the world to me throughout this journey and life.

My dearest friends—Jessica, Tina, Megan, Abi, Serene, Anaka, Alicia, Lena, Josh, and Mary—thank you for standing by my side through the ups and downs, all these years, and for being my pillars of strength. Your friendship has given me the courage to pursue my dreams.

Kim, who tirelessly styled our hair for all the beautiful photos featured in this book. Your talent brought my vision to life, and I am forever grateful for you and our friendship.

Brisa, who has always been there for me. Who also meticulously steamed the million outfits I had for the photoshoot for this book. Your meticulous attention to detail ensured that we looked our best. And for teaching me how to cook authentic Mexican dishes.

Meggie Moo, thank you for your invaluable assistance in bringing this cookbook to life. Your talent, creative input, and support have been instrumental in shaping this project into what it is today. Couldn't have done this without you!!!!!!

A special mention goes out to David, whose generosity allowed me the time and space to work on this book. Your understanding and willingness to take care of everything else while I poured my heart into these pages have been immeasurable. Thanks ba.

My online to IRL friends ~ Beth, Karina, Bree, Laura, Lisa, Marisa, Susan, Cathy, Ces, Erin, Jessica, Adela, Griselda, Megan, Stephanie, and all my ACE girls. You are my inspiration for being the best mommy. Thank you for supporting all of my crazy. Hehe :)

My friends and inspirations: Joanne, Matt, Jon, Dylan, Adam, Kevin, Lisa, Joyce, My, Michael, Fabby, Alexa, Jeenie, and Tinger.

Ms. Shannon Sheldon, thank you for taking over and making the aprons for me. I am truly grateful to have had you as my fashion design teacher and to have you in my life.

Super big thank you to Alix and Mack, for always keeping me on track and managing my workload. Your support and assistance through this have been invaluable, and I am deeply appreciative of your contributions. Thank you for always fighting for me and having my best interests in mind.

Of course ~ Ciarra, Lizzie, and Marcella. Ciarra, I'm so happy I found you. You absolutely brought my vision to life, and I loved working with you. Thank you, ladies, for busting your butts day in and day out with me for my new baby.

Olivia, Jessica, and the team at DK for believing in my ideas and truly letting me have creative freedom to make this cookbook the way I dreamed it to be. Thank you so much for your hard work and dedication to this book.

Thank you to the teams at Zwilling, OmieBox, Yumbox, Bento&co., Our Place, Caraway, and Bentgo for sending me your beautiful products to create this cookbook. Forever grateful.

Last but certainly not least, my deepest gratitude to Charlie. Your belief in me has been a constant source of inspiration. Thank you for providing me with the time and space I needed to work on this cookbook and for guiding me throughout the entire process.

It takes a village. Thank you all so much from the bottom of my heart! I love you!

ABOUT THE AUTHOR

Sulhee Jessica Woo, affectionately crowned the "Bento Box Queen," is a home chef, artist, and social media personality of Korean, Chinese, and Hawaiian heritage. She is a mother of three lovely girls and two chihuahua mixes and a proud member of the Asian American and Pacific Islander (AAPI) community.

Jessica gained popularity on social media platforms, such as TikTok and YouTube, due to her amazing talent for creating intricate and visually stunning bento boxes. Through her art, she showcases her love for food and creativity and her dedication to being a great mom. Jessica's influence extends beyond the kitchen; as an AAPI advocate, she leverages her online presence to foster cultural understanding and celebrate the richness of diverse identities. Her message is one of self-acceptance and she demonstrates the power of channeling one's unique traits into creative outlets.

Jessica's work has garnered attention from esteemed media entities, such as MBC, *The Los Angeles Times, Access Hollywood,* and *Good Morning America*, cementing her status as an ever-rising icon. Her story resonates deeply with the world, especially women and mothers who see in her a beacon of inspiration from her ability to nurture her family, pursue artistic endeavors, and cultivate a personal brand with grace and enthusiasm.

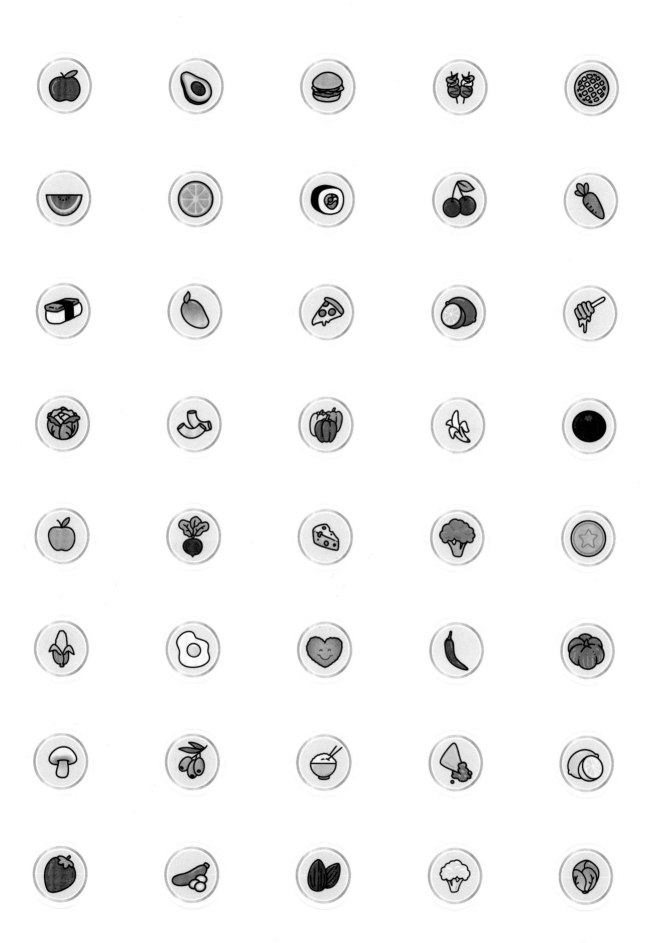

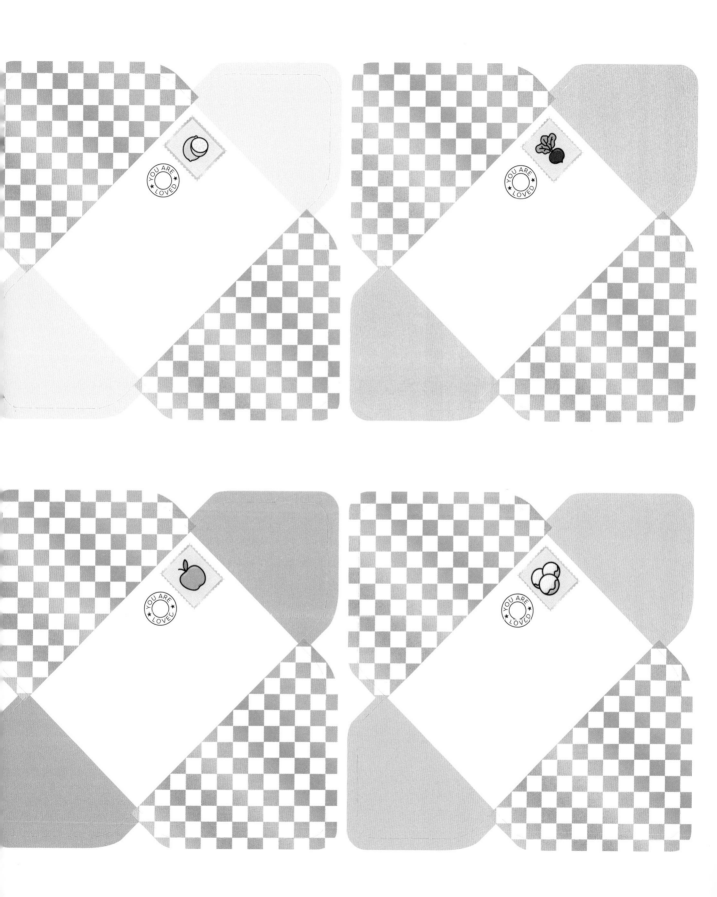

the C
Dinn...

Be Fabulous Today !!

...ugh a little harder, cry a little less, and smile a lot more.

I LOVE you!
- mama ♡

...ke ...ly ...KE ...S

I'm going to miss you so much while you're gone. come back home soon.

I'm so hap... got to me... all of you... ...eachers... ...e a gr...

...u can ...s, you ...ead!

THIS MAY SOUND CHEESY
THINK YOU'RE GRATE!

MOM   Maxine

This lunch was made with love by a loving mother for a loving child.

I Love you so much ...ly! xoxo you're

Hey ba... you're the greatest gift ever go...

Lo...

!

Everything you can imagine is real

Hi bubs. Hope you are feeling better today! I ♡ U!

I ♡ you with my whole entire heart ♡

Don't be a lady. Be a legend.
- stevie nicks

Hi baby! ♡ you are beautiful! and so smart! I love you!
xoxo

...y AAPI ...onth!

...f all the places, ...ould be... ...want ...re

I more day until winter...

Remember, ...t words